Mathematical Modeling
in the
Secondary School Curriculum

Mathematical Modeling
in the
Secondary School Curriculum

A Resource Guide of Classroom Exercises

Edited by

Frank Swetz
and
J. S. Hartzler

NATIONAL COUNCIL OF TEACHERS OF MATHEMATICS

Copyright © 1991 by
THE NATIONAL COUNCIL OF TEACHERS OF MATHEMATICS, INC.
1906 Association Drive, Reston, Virginia 22091 .
All rights reserved

Second printing 1994

Library of Congress Cataloging-in-Publication Data:

Mathematical modeling in the secondary school curriculum: a resource
  guide of classroom exercises / edited by Frank Swetz and J.S.
  Hartzler.
        p.   cm.
  A selected sample of exercises were originally presented at
workshops.
  Includes bibliographical references.
  ISBN 0-87353-306-2
  1. Mathematical models. 2. Mathematics—Study and teaching
(Secondary)   I. Swetz, Frank.   II. Hartzler, J. S. (Jefferson S.)
QA401.M39284   1991
511'.8'0712—dc20   90-25644
                                                               CIP

Printed in the United States of America

Table of Contents

*Indicates that computer programming activities are involved.

Preface

Increasingly over the past ten years, national conferences and committees investigating the state of American mathematics education have advocated an increased emphasis on problem solving and mathematical applications. In 1975, the Conference Board of the Mathematical Sciences (CBMS) issued its *Overview and Analysis of School Mathematics K–12,* which recommended the incorporation of mathematical applications and modeling situations into the secondary school curriculum (p. 145). Expressing similar concerns, the National Council of Teachers of Mathematics (NCTM), in setting goals for mathematics instruction for the decade of the 1980s, singled out problem solving as a focus of attention. The NCTM's *Agenda for Action* (1980) notes the need for providing mathematics teachers "experiences that develop their capacities in modeling and problem solving" (p. 5). In its *New Goals for Mathematical Sciences Education* (1984), the CBMS advised that the changing nature of mathematics required teachers to continually upgrade their knowledge and skills through advanced study and suggested mathematical modeling as an area of such study (p. 25). *Everybody Counts: A Report to the Nation on the Future of Mathematics Education,* published by the National Research Council in 1989, warns of an urgent need for teaching reforms that include an emphasis on model building (p. 83). More recently, the NCTM formulated a specific plan of action, *Curriculum and Evaluation Standards for School Mathematics* (1989), stressing the importance of mathematical modeling as a facet of problem solving. Despite these repeated recommendations and exhortations, however, little effort has been expended in preparing secondary school teachers to use mathematical modeling techniques and situations effectively in their classrooms.

For several years, the Mathematical Sciences Program of the Pennsylvania State University at Harrisburg has been working with secondary school mathematics teachers to implement modeling activities in the school curriculum. During the course of in-service workshops and, in particular, an NSF-sponsored Summer Honors Workshop called "Mathematical Modeling in the School Curriculum" (MMSC), a variety of classroom modeling activities were prepared and classroom tested. The sharing of successful learning/teaching activities is an important aspect of curriculum development work. This manual was prepared as a part of that sharing experience and is intended for a broad audience of mathematics teachers. Its contents examine the principles and techniques of mathematical modeling at the secondary school level. A selected sample of the successful classroom modeling exercises is enclosed. These exercises may be modified or used in toto as the reader sees fit. It is in the classroom incorporation of such exercises that the concepts and use of mathematical modeling truly emerge.

Many people contributed to the development of this manual; we would like to formally recognize and acknowledge them for their contributions. A heartfelt thanks to all the teachers and students who learned with us about mathematical modeling—especially those teachers who contributed directly to the exercises in this manual: Wayne Bradburn, Rosemarie Dowger, Thomas Evitts, Lynn Godshall, Christine Lauer, Donna Medeiros, Jeff Moral, Linda O'Connor, Robert Tate, and Georgia Voegler. Ellen Shatto, who was a staff member for the 1987 MMSC Workshop, assisted in compiling the Bibliography, aided teachers in developing their models, and contributed a model of her own to this manual. Another colleague, Ali Bakht, improved the computer programs used, and Elsie Wilt and Mimi Wasilewski typed the manuscript.

Introduction to Mathematical Modeling

IN CONSIDERING or attempting any curriculum change, one may have many questions: Exactly what does the change concern? Why is it beneficial? How much more work must I do? How can it be accomplished? The material that follows may help answer these questions.

What is mathematical modeling?

Intuitively, most people understand what a *model* is in the physical sense. It is a replication, usually scaled down, of an object. Children make model boats or airplanes. The model shares many of the properties of the original object: it may have the same features, may be the same color, and may even function similarly to the object it represents. For example, a model sailboat can float and is propelled by the wind. The model is convenient for work or play precisely because it does not share all the properties of the "parent" object. Properties such as size and weight can prevent us from working with a real object, whereas its model can be easily handled. A model can be manipulated and studied, and in the process, information on the parent object can be obtained. The aeronautical features of a supersonic passenger plane can be determined by using models in a wind tunnel. The alternative test strategy—building a full-scale plane and testing it in a wind tunnel—would be cost-prohibitive. Physical models are a valuable tool in many fields of technological and industrial research.

Theoretical models can also be constructed. A theoretical model of an object or phenomenon is a set of rules or laws that accurately represents that object or phenomenon in the mind of an observer. When those rules or laws are mathematical in nature, a mathematical model has been developed. Thus, *a mathematical model is a mathematical structure that approximates the features of a phenomenon. The process of devising a mathematical model is called mathematical modeling.* Some basic mathematical structures that lend themselves to modeling are graphs, equations (formulas) or systems of equations or inequalities, digraphs, index numbers, numerical tables, and algorithms. For a civil engineer, the amount of deflection (bending) of a beam under a load is important. One could set up a beam, subject it to a load, and measure its deflection; however, this process would be time consuming and expensive. It would be more convenient if a theoretical model for a beam under a load existed. Through experimentation, observation, and calculation, such a model was determined:

1

$$\text{Deflection} = \frac{PL^3}{48EI}$$

where L = the length of the beam;

      P = the load;

      E = the modulus of elasticity, which depends on the material from which the beam is made;

      I = the moment of inertia, which depends on the cross-sectional area of the beam.

In this instance, the model for deflection is a single equation. Most significant formulas are really mathematical models of the phenomenon described.

What is the difference between problem solving and mathematical modeling?

Mathematical modeling is a type of problem solving. Even among mathematics educators, the term *problem solving* means different things to different people. Certainly, the computational exercises students do in class are a form of problem solving—a problem exists, and a correct answer must be found. Most frequently, however, when teachers think of problem solving, they think of obtaining solutions to word problems where students must interpret what the problem requires and then decide how to find an answer. Word problems are more demanding in their requirements than computation exercises. For other teachers, problem solving may suggest the unraveling and solution of puzzle problems, such as the magic square and the Tower of Hanoi. Although mathematical modeling shares characteristics with all these problem-solving situations, it is distinctly different. Frequently, in a mathematical modeling situation, a phenomenon that is seemingly nonmathematical in context must be modeled. This may be an event in the realm of politics, such as predicting election results; of economics, such as finding the long-term behavior of oil prices; or even of ecology, such as predicting the future growth patterns of a forest. These events should be interpreted as problems. Important factors must be discerned, relationships must be determined, and these relationships must be mathematically interpreted. The mathematical interpretations of relationships allow for an analysis of the phenomenon so that conclusions (solutions) can be found. Thus, mathematical modeling is a systematic process that draws on many skills and employs the higher cognitive activities of interpretation, analysis, and synthesis. The modeling process is composed of four main stages:

1. Observing a phenomenon, delineating the problem situation inherent in the phenomenon, and discerning the important factors (variables/parameters) that affect the problem

2. Conjecturing the relationships among factors and interpreting them mathematically to obtain a model for the phenomenon
3. Applying appropriate mathematical analysis to the model
4. Obtaining results and reinterpreting them in the context of the phenomenon under study and drawing conclusions

These stages can be schematically represented in the form of a closed cycle (fig. 1).

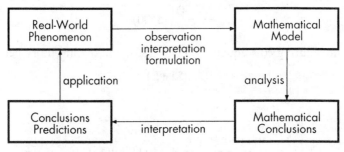

Fig. 1

A fifth stage could also be added to this process—the testing and refinement of the model. Are the conclusions usable? Do they make sense? If not, a reexamination of the model's factors and structure is called for and a possible reformulation of the model may be necessary.

As an example of a modeling process, consider the situation where a manufacturer must produce 100 000 units of an item in a year. Although he may manufacture the items periodically over a year's time, he is seeking an optimum schedule of production that will minimize costs. The primary costs in question are the following: (S) production set-up costs, $500 for each production run; (M) manufacturing costs per unit, $5; ($I$) annual inventory or storage costs per unit, $1. Of course, production schedules can be set up in many ways. For example, one huge production run can be performed at the beginning of the year; this schedule will cut down on production costs but raise storage or inventory costs. Several production runs will increase production costs but decrease inventory costs. Which strategy will result in the greatest economic savings for the manufacturer? We seek a relationship between costs and the number of production runs, thus identifying the problem. Can a mathematical equation or formula be derived relating total cost to the number of production runs? Let L represent lot size, that is, the number of units manufactured in each production run, $0 < L \le 100\ 000$. Assume an ideal situation where a newly made lot is put into inventory and used up at a uniform rate. At this rate the inventory decreases to zero by the time another lot is manufactured. Under this assumption, the average inventory can be represented by $L/2$. Using the designated parameters and representing cost as a function of lot size, $C(L)$, we get

$$C(L) = (\text{set-up cost}) + (\text{manufacturing cost}) + (\text{inventory cost}),$$

where the number of lots to be undertaken in a year is given by

$$\frac{100\ 000}{L}.$$

Then the set-up cost becomes

$$\frac{100\ 000}{L}\ (\$500),$$

the manufacturing cost equals $(100\ 000)\ (\$5)$, and the inventory becomes

$$\frac{(\$1)(L)}{2}.$$

Thus,

$$C(L) = \frac{(100\ 000)(\$500)}{L} + (100\ 000)(\$5) + \frac{(\$1)(L)}{2}.$$

A model, in this example an equation, is thus established. Now for the analysis of the cost and lot-size problem. How does cost behave in relation to lot size? Since cost is composed of a fixed cost, $500\ 000, and a variable cost for manufacture and storage, only the behavior of the variable cost needs to be studied. This can be done in several ways: a table of computed values can be made (fig. 2), or a graph can be constructed (fig. 3).

L (1000s)	C (L) ($)	L	C(L)
5	12 500	55	28 409
10	10 000	60	30 083
15	10 833	65	33 269
20	12 500	70	35 714
25	14 500	75	38 167
30	16 667	80	40 625
35	18 929	85	43 088
40	21 250	90	45 889
45	23 611	95	48 026
50	26 000	100	50 500

Fig. 2

From either the table or the graph it can be determined that cost will be minimized when lots of 10 000 units are produced. Using this figure, we find $100\ 000/10\ 000 = 10$ lots a year, or $365/10$, are required—a lot every 37 days. The mathematical analysis could have been performed using cal-

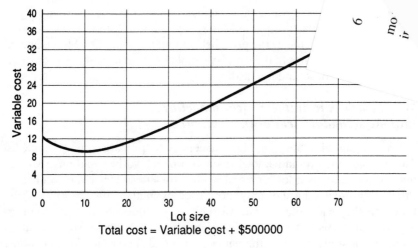

Fig. 3

culus. In minimizing $C(L)$, we find

$$C'(L) = \frac{-50 \times 10^6}{L^2} + \frac{1}{2} = 0,$$

or

$$L = \sqrt{(2)(50)(10^6)} = 10\ 000 \text{ units.}$$

Since

$$C''(L) = \frac{(2)(50) \times 10^6}{L^3} > 0,$$

10 000 units result in a minimum value for $C(L)$. In this situation, note that if the manufacturer chose to make all the items in one lot rather than the optimal ten lots, he would have incurred an additional $40 500 in costs!

Does mathematical modeling mostly involve discrete mathematics?

No. Although many phenomena can be modeled by using concepts from discrete mathematics, such as digraphs, finite matrix algorithms, or Markov chains, modeling is certainly not restricted to this type of mathematics. The manufacturing situation previously examined did not depend on discrete mathematics. It involved the derivation and investigation of a simple function. Mathematical modeling can be accomplished using a variety of mathematical concepts and skills: geometric, algebraic, trigonometric, probabilistic, and analytic. Certainly, most of the mathematical topics taught at the secondary school level can lend themselves to the development of specific models. Linear equations and inequalities are particularly useful in many eling situations. Graphs and simple proportions are easy models to interpret. The quadratic equation can serve as a basis for understanding the dynamics of a projectile or the price behavior of a commodity. Mathematical modeling demonstrates that even very simple mathematics, if used constructively, can have profound applications.

Why incorporate mathematical modeling into the secondary school curriculum?

One of our ultimate goals as teachers is to prepare young people to function confidently and knowledgeably in real-world situations. Mathematical modeling is a form of real-world problem solving. The techniques previously discussed are exactly those used by mathematicians to solve the problems they encounter in their workplace. A modeling approach to problem solving focuses a variety of mathematical skills on finding a solution and helps a student see mathematics in a broad spectrum of applications. The strategies and skills learned in modeling exercises are easily transferable to new situations. Students involved in modeling experiences obtain a greater appreciation of the power of mathematics. As one student in a first-year algebra class commented after doing a modeling exercise, "Now that's real mathematics!"

How can mathematical modeling be incorporated into secondary school mathematics teaching?

Mathematical modeling can be incorporated in many ways. Separate courses or sections of a course devoted exclusively to mathematical modeling are not necessary. The separation or isolation of mathematical modeling from the rest of the mathematics curriculum tends to raise the suspicion in the minds of students that mathematical modeling is something unusual or difficult. A modeling approach to problem solving and modeling theory should be incorporated gradually in a low-key manner into the existing curriculum. Many of the problem situations and relevant mathematics are already in place; they need only a slightly different solution orientation to become modeling situations.

How can a teacher prepare to undertake modeling exercises with students?

Teachers should learn about mathematical modeling by reading more on the subject. A selected bibliography is enclosed for this purpose. The *Mathematics Teacher* has carried some excellent articles on mathematical modeling. Examine the enclosed modeling exercises that were prepared by fellow teachers for classroom use. Choose one or two exercises that are appropriate for your teaching situation and go through them. Try the mathematics. Does the problem approach make sense? Do you think your students would like to try such exercises? We hope your answers to the last two questions are in the affirmative. If so, you should attempt some of the prepared exercises with your students. As you gain confidence with the ideas and techniques of mathematical modeling, you can find other appropriate modeling situations or devise your own.

Classroom Modeling Exercises

The following selection of classroom modeling exercises has been developed and classroom tested by secondary school teachers. These examples of modeling exercises have been used with students successfully to explain the concepts and the methods of problem solving by using mathematical modeling. A variety of modeling situations are considered, including the development of functions, graphical analysis, and the use of algorithmic procedures.

All exercises basically follow the same format: a problem is stated, a model is developed to solve the problem, the model is applied to the problem, and the result is noted and discussed. The intended grade level of participation is noted on the title page along with the required principal mathematics concepts. This information is summarized on the descriptive list of exercises given in figure 4. Some exercises will introduce new mathematical concepts that are not usually found in the secondary school curriculum. Every exercise has a teacher's guide, in which the author shares his or her experiences with the model and gives some teaching advice. These guides are found in the Appendix. Some exercises are self-directed and student-oriented, whereas others approximate lesson plans and are intended for teacher consultation and action. These exercises can be copied and used in toto or modified. Where necessary, computer programs are supplied.

Try mathematical modeling in your classroom. Use these exercises. Both you and your students may like the experience.

LIST OF EXERCISES

Exercise Number	Appropriate Subject Level[1]	Principal Concepts and Skills[2]
1	General Mathematics	Ratio and proportion
2	General Mathematics	Pythagorean formula
3	General Mathematics	Distance formula
4	General Mathematics	Probability
5	Algebra 1	Simple graphing

[Continued on next page]

LIST OF EXERCISES—*Continued*

6	Algebra 1	Graphing, area computation
7	Algebra 1	Inequalities
8	Algebra 1	Functions, pattern recognition
9	Algebra 1	Algebraic operations
10	Algebra 1	Simple programming
11	Algebra 2	Linear inequalities, graphing
12	Algebra 2	Circle equation
13	Algebra 2	Arithmetic series
14	Algebra 2	Permutations, counting techniques
15	Algebra 2	Linear and parabolic equations, programming
16	Algebra 2	Basic trigonometric functions
17	Algebra 2	Velocity and acceleration formulas
18	Algebra 2	Exponential functions
19	Algebra 2	Linear and parabolic equations, graphing
20	Algebra 2	Basic trigonometric functions, programming
21	Algebra 2	Matrix arithmetic
22	Precalculus	Transcendental functions

1. The suggested level represents the lower limit of mathematical involvement. For example, if the exercise is designated for algebra 1, students who have passed beyond algebra 1 could also undertake the exercise.

2. The listing indicates the most advanced topic involved.

Fig. 4

1

WILDLIFE POPULATION SURVEY

Description of the problem

The game commission would like to know the number of fish in a pond. This information would be valuable for stocking the pond and for studying the availability of fish in the pond. How would you approximate the size of the pond's fish population?

Mathematics concepts required: Arithmetic (ratio and proportion)

Appropriate for students in: General mathematics

Model

We do not know the number of fish in the pond. Let the unknown size of the fish population be n. Assume that we are allowed to catch some fish, place plastic tags on their tails in a way that will not hurt them, and then release them back into the pond. Suppose we catch and tag p number of fish and return them to the pond. We let these fish settle back into pond life, and we return several days later to catch another quantity of fish, q. Some of these fish bear the tags we put on them a few days earlier. Let the number of these tagged fish be represented by x. Then using simple proportions, we may conclude that

$$\frac{p}{n} = \frac{x}{q} \,.$$

Since we want to estimate the size of n, we can solve this equation for n, obtaining

$$n = \frac{pq}{x} \,.$$

How can we refine this technique to obtain a more accurate estimate? Fish move about a pond freely; therefore, we should sample the fish population in several different areas and obtain the arithmetic mean of the x's in each catch, $\bar{x}$. Then a more accurate formula for the estimate n would be

$$n = \frac{pq}{\bar{x}} \,.$$

This procedure of estimating wildlife populations is called the capture/recapture method and is used by game and conservation officials.

Example

Assume that in a certain pond you catch, tag, and release ten fish. Then you apply the capture/recapture method and obtain the following data:

Sample catch	Number of tagged fish x	Size of sample catch q
1	3	15
2	0	15
3	3	15
4	1	15
5	2	15
6	4	15
7	6	15
8	2	15
9	4	15
10	2	15

Solving for n, we get the following:

After 5 catches	After 10 catches
$\dfrac{1.8}{15} = \dfrac{10}{n}$	$\dfrac{2.7}{15} = \dfrac{10}{n}$
$83 = n$	$56 = n$

The actual count of fish in the pond was 80.

Student assignment

1. Each group of students will receive a shoe box (pond) with an unspecified number of one-inch paper squares (fish), $n < 100$.
2. Each group of students should then "go fishing" and select 10 squares, mark them, and return them to the box.
3. Shake the box, select a number of squares (fish), say 15. Record the number of marked ones and then return all of them to the box.
4. Shake the box and repeat, completing the table below:

    (Number of fish in the box: n Number of fish tagged: 10)

Sample catch	Number of tagged fish x	Size of sample catch q
1		
2		
3		
4		
5		
6		
7		
8		
9		
10		

Total

5. Estimate the number of fish in the pond. Count the fish to see how close the estimate is to the actual amount.
6. Are you pleased with the estimate? How accurate is it?
7. Suppose a pond contains three types of fish: blue gills, bass, and catfish. Estimate the number in each population, that is, estimate how many blue gills, bass, and catfish are in the pond. Adapt the capture/recapture procedure to accomplish this task.

2

PACK THEM IN!

Description of the problem

A manufacturing company needs to find short-term storage for some cylindrical containers. The company wants to do this at minimum expense. Therefore, the job is to pack them in using as little storage space as possible.

The containers are right circular cylinders with a radius of one foot and a height of three feet. All 175 containers must be stored in an upright position. Storage is required for two months.

Storage units are available for rent in three sizes: 11 feet × 11 feet for $67 a month; 11 feet × 22 feet for $105 a month; 11 feet × 33 feet for $130 a month. All units are 10 feet high.

Pack them in!

Mathematics concepts required: Pythagorean theorem

Appropriate for students in: General mathematics

Model

The decision of how to store the containers can be made by finding out how many containers will fit into each storage area. How many in each row? How many rows? How many layers?

The problem of cylindrical containers is compounded by the fact that the storage pattern can be adjusted in one of two ways. Containers can be lined

12

up in identical rows, or they can be staggered in rows in order to take advantage of their circular bases.

A chart will help to organize the information and provide a basis for considering the costs involved in the rental of the storage space. Charts are provided at the end of the problem.

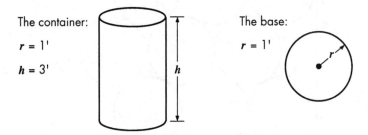

The container:

$r = 1'$

$h = 3'$

The base:

$r = 1'$

• If the containers are aligned in identical rows, viewed from the top the pattern looks like figure 2.1.

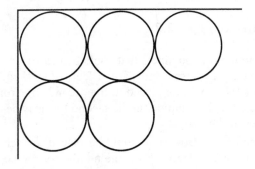

Fig. 2.1

Using the pattern in figure 2.1

1. Find the number of containers that could be placed across the back of each storage area whose lengths are 11 feet, 22 feet, and 33 feet. This is the number of containers per row.
2. Find the number of rows that could be placed in each storage area. Each area is 11 feet deep. This is the number of rows of containers.
3. Find the number of layers of containers that could be placed in each storage area. Each area is 10 feet high.
4. Record the information on chart 1. Calculate the total number of containers that would fit into each area. Then determine the number of storage units needed and the cost of storage for two months.

• If the containers are staggered in rows, the pattern looks like figure 2.2.

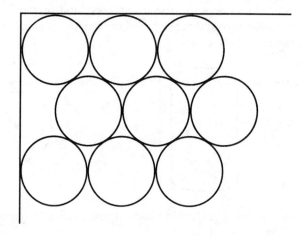

Fig. 2.2

Using the pattern in figure 2.2

1. Find the number of containers that could be placed across the back of each storage area whose lengths are 11 feet, 22 feet, and 33 feet. Find the number that could be placed in the second row from the back of the storage area. The number in the second row may be different from the number in the first row.

2. Find the number of rows that could be placed in each storage area. Each area is 11 feet deep. This is the number of rows of containers.

3. Find the number of layers of containers that could be placed in each storage area. Each area is 10 feet high.

4. Record this information on chart 2. Calculate the total number of containers that would fit into each area. Then determine the number of units needed and the cost of storage for two months.

Chart 1: Identical row alignment

Unit	Cost per month	Number per row	Rows	Layers	Total	Units Needed	Cost for two months
11 × 11							
11 × 22							
11 × 33							

Chart 2: Staggered row alignment

Unit	Cost per month	Number per row	Rows	Layers	Total	Units Needed	Cost for two months
11 × 11							
11 × 22							
11 × 33							

Student assignment

1. From the information in your charts, what appears to be the least expensive way to store the containers?
2. Would your decision be the same if the restriction of storing the containers in an upright position were removed?
3. What is the second-best choice?

3

COST OF A LONG-DISTANCE TELEPHONE CALL

Description of the problem

Find the cost of making a three-minute telephone call from Harrisburg, Pa., to Pittsburgh, Pa., at 3:00 P.M. on a Tuesday.

The cost of a long-distance telephone call is based on airline distance between the two exchanges. A grid system helps to determine this distance. Cost charts from phone companies help determine the cost of the call. You can find the distance between exchanges and then use cost charts to determine the cost of this long-distance phone call.

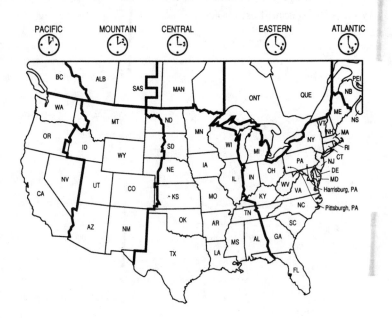

Mathematics concepts required: The distance formula

Appropriate for students in: General mathematics

Model

On 7 February 1960 the Bell telephone system began using a new method to determine the rate mileage on long-distance telephone calls between two states. It has been in use on interstate, private-line service since May 1959.

16

Now it will also apply to calls between points in the United States and Canada.

Since 1960, the calculation of the cost of a long-distance phone call requires the use of a new theory of map making developed by the company's Long Lines Department: an improved method for determining airline distance between two telephone exchanges. One advantage of this new method is that distances measured between areas are more precise.

The second group of three digits of any phone number is known as the *exchange*.

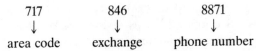

It was impractical to make up a table of distances between all possible exchanges in Canada and the United States. The telephone company's new method of finding the distance between two exchanges is called the *Vertical-Horizontal Coordinate System*, or the *V-H System*. The company superimposed a series of vertical and horizontal lines over the map of the two countries (fig. 3.1).

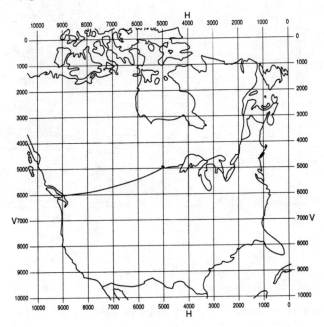

Fig. 3.1

The newly developed square-grid system uses straight lines on a flat map surface (differing from the curved lines of latitude and longitude on the earth's spherical surface). The square grid is divided into 100 large squares. The upper-right corner is called the *origin of the system*. Each of the 100 squares has a length and width of 1000 units. The V-H System assigns an ordered pair to each exchange area on the map. The first coordinate of the ordered pair is called the *vertical coordinate* (the number associated with the vertical line through the exchange area) and the second is called the *horizontal coordinate* (the number associated with the horizontal line through the exchange area). These are referred to as the *V* and *H coordinates*.

Each large square (scaled to 1000 units each side) is divided into ten smaller squares. (See fig. 3.2.) This division makes it possible to assign more accurate *V* and *H* coordinates.

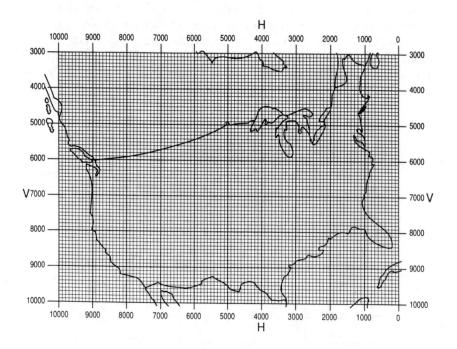

Fig. 3.2

The Long Lines Department isolated one small square and found that its side actually represented $\frac{1}{\sqrt{10}}$ of a mile, or 0.3162 mile. Each locality is assigned a pair of *V* and *H* coordinates. Several locations, along with their *V* and *H* coordinates, are listed in table 3.1. A complete list of these coordinates can be found in the Local and Joint Tariffs Manual, Pa. PUC Toll No. 1A, 1D, 2C at the Bell Telephone Company.

Using these coordinates, you can calculate airline distance between two exchanges as follows:

1. Compute the difference between the V coordinates of the two exchanges. Then compute the difference between the H coordinates. The difference is the absolute value of one V coordinate minus the other, or one H coordinate minus the other.

2. Square the differences.

3. Add the squares of the two differences.

4. Take the square root of this result. Round to the next higher whole number if a fractional amount results. This number is the distance between the two exchanges as expressed in coordinate numbers.

5. Multiply this result by 0.3162, the mileage scale factor for coordinate readings. The number obtained is the mileage between exchanges. Since fractional miles are considered full miles, increase the mileage by 1 if a fractional mile is obtained.

In the sample problem, find the airline distance between the exchanges for Harrisburg and Pittsburgh as follows:

$$\text{Harrisburg} \quad (5363, 1733)$$
$$\text{Pittsburgh} \quad (5621, 2185)$$

1. V: $\quad\quad\quad\quad\quad\quad\quad\quad\quad\quad$ $5621 - 5363 = 258$
   H: $\quad\quad\quad\quad\quad\quad\quad\quad\quad\quad$ $2185 - 1733 = 452$

2. Differences squared: $\quad\quad\quad$ $(258)^2 = 66\,564$
   $\quad\quad\quad\quad\quad\quad\quad\quad\quad\quad\quad$ $(452)^2 = 204\,304$

3. Sum of squares: $\quad\quad\quad$ $66\,564 + 204\,304 = 270\,868$

4. Squareroot: $\quad\quad\quad\quad\quad\quad$ $\sqrt{270\,868} = 520.4498$
   Round: $\quad\quad\quad\quad\quad\quad\quad\quad\quad$ 521

5. Multiply by 0.3162: $\quad\quad\quad$ $(521)(0.3162) = 164.7402$
   Round: $\quad\quad\quad\quad\quad\quad\quad\quad\quad$ 165

Let us look at the method of computing airline distance more closely. In general, represent the vertical and horizontal coordinates of the two exchanges by x and y, respectively.

$\quad\quad$ Exchange 1: $\quad\quad\quad\quad\quad\quad\quad\quad$ (x_1, y_1)
$\quad\quad$ Exchange 2: $\quad\quad\quad\quad\quad\quad\quad\quad$ (x_2, y_2)

According to the first four steps of the five-step process:

1. Compute the differences between the
   V and H coordinates: $\quad\quad\quad\quad\quad\quad$ $x_2 - x_1 \quad\quad y_2 - y_1$

2. Square the differences: $(x_2 - x_1)^2$ $(y_2 - y_1)^2$

3. Add the squares of the two differences: $(x_2 - x_1)^2 + (y_2 - y_1)^2$

4. Take the square root of this result: $\sqrt{(x_2 - x_1)^2 + (y_2 - y_1)^2}$

You should recognize this as a familiar formula. What is its name?

Once the mileage between two exchanges is known, you can refer to the cost charts established by telephone companies to determine the cost of your long-distance phone call. Most companies have day, evening, and night/weekend rates. The evening and night/weekend rates reflect discounts furnished by the phone companies.

The calling cost between two exchanges, once the distance is known, is determined as follows:

1. Locate the distance in the rate mileage column of the chart.
2. Determine the rate period for the phone call:

Day	8 A.M.–5 P.M., Monday through Friday
Evening	5 P.M.–11 P.M., Sunday through Friday
Night/Weekend	11 P.M.–8 P.M. daily all day Saturday Sunday until 5 P.M.

3. Read the cost for the first minute and then multiply the additional minute cost by the number of additional minutes of the phone call (fractional amounts of time are considered full minutes).
4. Add these two costs to determine the total cost of the phone call.

In the sample problem, use the ITT chart to determine the cost of a three-minute long-distance phone call from Harrisburg to Pittsburgh during the day-rate period.

1. The distance was found to be 165 miles. Locate 165 miles in the distance column.
2. Day rates are listed.
3. Initial minute: .324
   Two additional minutes: 2 (.259) = .518
4. Add and round up these costs: .324 + .518 = .842 = .85

Therefore, the day-rate cost of a three-minute long-distance phone call between Harrisburg and Pittsburgh is $0.85.

Student assignment

1. Use table 3.1 to compute airline distance between the following ex-changes:

    a. York, Pa., and Lancaster, Pa.
    b. Gettysburg, Pa., and Philadelphia, Pa.
    c. Dover, Pa., and Ocean City, Md.
    d. Millersville, Pa., and Orlando, Fla.
    e. Red Lion, Pa., and Montreal, Quebec
    f. Baltimore, Md., and New York, N.Y.

2. Use the MCI cost chart (fig. 3.3) to find the cost of the following phone calls:

    a. A 6-minute call from York to Lancaster at 3:00 P.M. on Saturday
    b. A 15-minute call from Gettysburg to Philadelphia at 10:00 A.M. on Friday
    c. A 23-minute call from Dover to Ocean City at 7:00 P.M. on Sunday

3. Use the ITT cost chart (fig. 3.4) to find the cost of the following phone calls:

    a. A 10-minute call from Millersville to Orlando at 6:00 P.M. on Monday
    b. A 13-minute call from Red Lion to Montreal at 2:00 P.M. on Thursday
    c. A 20-minute call from Baltimore to New York City at 5:15 P.M. on Saturday

4. Compute the airline distance between York and State College. What is the distance? _____
    Use MCI and ITT cost charts to compute the cost of a 15-minute long-distance phone call on Wednesday at 4:00 P.M. Compare the costs.

    MCI: $_____
    ITT: $_____

TABLE 3.1

	V coordinate	H coordinate
Pennsylvania		
Allentown	5166	1585
Bloomsburg	5191	1769
Dover	5407	1695
Elizabethtown	5356	1680
Gettysburg	5474	1727
Harrisburg	5363	1733
Hershey	5337	1704
Lancaster	5348	1626
Lock Haven	5260	1919
Millersville	5358	1629
Philadelphia	5251	1458
Pittsburgh	5621	2185
Pocono Lake	5077	1651
Red Lion	5402	1650
Shippensburg	5461	1794
State College	5360	1933
York	5402	1674
Baltimore, Md.	5510	1575
Ocean City, Md.	5532	1241
Atlantic City, N.J.	5284	1284
New York, N.Y.	4997	1406
Orlando, Fla.	7954	1031
Los Angeles, Calif.	9213	7878
Montreal, Quebec	4127	1992
Niagara Falls, Ontario	5055	2379
Toronto, Ontario	4981	2488
Cancún, Mexico	9683	4098

Cost Chart: Pennsylvania Intrastate Rates (MCI)

Mileage	Day Rate		Evening		Night/Weekend	
	1st min.	Add. min.	1st min.	Add. min.	1st min.	Add. min.
1–10	$.310	$.168	$.225	$.119	$.177	$.096
11–16	.310	.168	.225	.119	.177	.096
17–22	.320	.178	.233	.129	.183	.099
23–30	.360	.208	.263	.149	.207	.119
31–40	.380	.218	.278	.158	.219	.126
41–55	.400	.228	.293	.166	.231	.129
56–70	.410	.248	.300	.179	.237	.144
71–124	.420	.267	.308	.196	.243	.155
125–196	.430	.277	.315	.203	.249	.159
197–292	.440	.297	.323	.218	.255	.173
293–354	.450	.317	.330	.233	.261	.185

Fig. 3.3

Cost Chart: Pennsylvania Intrastate Rates (ITT)

Per-minute rates

The following rates apply to calls terminated at points within the contiguous United States, Washington, D.C., Puerto Rico, the U.S., Virgin Islands, Alaska, and Hawaii.

Mileage Band	Day Rate		Evening		Night/Weekend	
	1st min.	Add. min.	1st min.	Add. min.	1st min.	Add. min.
1–10	$.224	$.149	$.130	$.092	$.094	$.070
11–22	.274	.189	.160	.117	.120	.088
23–55	.304	.209	.184	.129	.134	.098
56–124	.324	.239	.192	.148	.142	.112
125–292	.324	.259	.194	.160	.142	.121
293–430	.334	.279	.198	.173	.144	.131
431–925	.354	.299	.209	.185	.154	.140
926–1910	.364	.309	.214	.191	.159	.145
1911–3000	.394	.319	.234	.197	.174	.149
3001–4250	.434	.349	.258	.216	.194	.164
4251–5750	.454	.369	.274	.228	.204	.173

Fig. 3.4

4

THE GROCERY STORE PROBLEM

Description of the problem

A small grocery store must decide whether to operate two check-out lines with one cashier at each line or one check-out line with one cashier and one bagger. With one cashier at each of two check-out lines, the average service time is two minutes a customer. With a cashier and a bagger at one check-out line, the average service time is one minute a shopper.

Mathematics background required: Elementary probability, random number concept

Appropriate for students in: General mathematics

Model

When a mathematical structure for a problem is difficult to obtain, often experimentation can be used to solve the problem. However, actual experimentation may be expensive or may lead to undesirable consequences, such as loss of customers. Simulation is a useful alternative to actual experimentation.

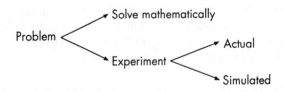

For the grocery store problem, simulation requires a numerical description of the grocery store check-out system for each minute of a part of a day for each check-out arrangement. The numerical description must include the number of customers served and the number waiting to be served. Random numbers will be used to indicate how many customers arrive at the check-out area at the beginning of each minute.

The decision of which arrangement to use will be based on the average customer waiting and service time in the check-out system. Since space is limited in the check-out region, the manager is also interested in the average line length.

A two-digit random-number table or random-number generator can be used to produce a sequence of numbers from the list {00, 01, 02, . . . , 98, 99}. A random sequence is one in which no pattern exists for the prediction of the next number in the sequence. One random number will be assigned to each minute of the simulation period.

As shown in table 4.1, if one of the forty numbers (00, 01, 02, . . . , 39) appears, we will assume that zero customers arrived during that minute. If one of the thirty numbers (40, 41, . . . , 69) appears, we will assume that one customer arrived; if one of the thirty numbers (70, 71, . . . , 99) appears, we will assume that two customers arrived. This arrangement is useful because the chance of a number from the list (00, 01, 02, . . . , 39) appearing is 40/100, which is the same as the observed fraction of minutes when zero customers actually arrived. A similar explanation holds for one and two arrivals.

TABLE 4.1

Number of arrivals at the check-out area per minute	Percentage of time	Random numbers assigned
0	40	00–39
1	30	40–69
2	30	70–99

The actual arrival of customers in the store is mimicked by the simulation process. A mathematical replica of the check-out process has been developed! (See table 4.2.)

The first column of the simulation table for the one-check-out system lists the minute numbers 1 to 30. The second column is a listing of thirty two-digit random numbers and should be completely filled from a random-number table before the rest of the table is finished. Column 3 records how many customers arrived and should be finished by using table 4.1. The balance of the simulation table is completed one row at a time, starting from the top. It is assumed that the customers arrive at the *beginning* of each minute.

To complete row 1, we observe that two persons arrive at the beginning of minute 1. These customers are labeled #1 and #2, and their arrival is recorded in the fourth column. Customer #1 is served immediately, and customer #2 must wait during the first minute, which places the entries in columns 5, 6, 7.

For minute 25, two persons numbered 18 and 19 arrive. By looking at minute 24, we see that customer 17 is waiting to be served. At the beginning of minute 25, customer 17 moves to the check-out area and customers 18 and 19 wait during the 25th minute, which places the 2 in column 7.

TABLE 4.2
One Checkout

Min. number	Random number	Number of arrivals	Customer arriving	Customer being served	Customer waiting	Total min. waiting
1	81	2	#1,2	#1	#2	1
2	02	0	—	2	—	0
3	60	1	3	3	—	0
4	04	0	—	—	—	0
5	46	1	4	4	—	0
6	31	0	—	—	—	0
7	67	1	5	5	—	0
8	25	0	—	—	—	0
9	24	0	—	—	—	0
10	10	0	—	—	—	0
11	40	1	6	6	—	0
12	02	0	—	—	—	0
13	39	0	—	—	—	0
14	68	1	7	7	—	0
15	08	0	—	—	—	0
16	59	1	8	8	—	0
17	66	1	9	9	—	0
18	90	2	10,11	10	11	1
19	12	0	—	11	—	0
20	64	1	12	12	—	0
21	79	2	13,14	13	14	1
22	31	0	—	14	—	0
23	86	2	15,16	15	16	1
24	68	1	17	16	17	1
25	82	2	18,19	17	18,19	2
26	89	2	20,21	18	19,20,21	3
27	80	2	22,23	19	20,21,22,23	4
28	11	0	—	20	21,22,23	3
29	62	1	24	21	22,23,24	3
30	16	0	—	22	23,24	2

After the table is completed, the required statistics are found. Average waiting time is calculated for the 22 customers who have passed through the system during the 30-minute period. The total waiting time for those 22 customers can be found by adding the numbers in column 7 and subtracting the 6 minutes waited by customers 23 and 24, who were still waiting at the end of the 30-minute period.

The average line length is obtained by dividing the total customer minutes of waiting time (22) by the number of minutes in the simulation (30) to yield an average waiting line length of 0.73 customer.

$$\text{Average waiting time (excluding service)} = \frac{16}{22} \simeq 0.73 \text{ min/customer}$$

$$\text{Average waiting time (including service)} = \frac{38}{22} \simeq 1.73 \text{ min/customer}$$

(*Note:* Only persons served during the thirty-minute interval are counted in these calculations.)

$$\text{Average line length} = 2230 \simeq 0.73 \text{ customer minutes/minute}$$
$$\text{(waiting for service)}$$
$$= 0.73 \text{ customer}$$

Comparable reasoning is used to find the entries in the simulation table for two checkouts (see table 4.3).

$$\text{Average waiting time (excluding service)} = \frac{12}{21} \simeq 0.57 \text{ min/customer}$$

$$\text{Average waiting time (including service)} = \frac{54}{21} \simeq 2.57 \text{ min/customer}$$

(*Note:* Only persons who have been completely served during the 30-minute interval are counted in these calculations.)

$$\text{Average line length} = \frac{21}{30} \simeq 0.70 \text{ customer minutes/minute}$$
$$= 0.70 \text{ customer}$$

Conclusion. Because the total average waiting time is shorter in the first system, it is preferred on the basis of this 30-minute simulation. A longer simulation will yield more reliable results.

Suggestions for further study and potential extensions

In a large automobile service center, mechanics go to the parts counter when a part is needed. There is an economic penalty for the company when mechanics have to wait in line, and there is a penalty if the parts counter is overstaffed. Simulation can be used to find the best staffing arrangement for the parts counter if information is available on arrivals and service rates at the parts counter.

TABLE 4.3
Two Checkouts

Min. number	Random number	Number of arrivals	Customer arriving	Line #1	Line #2	Customer waiting	Total min. waiting
1	81	2	#1,2	#1	#2	#—	0
2	02	0	—	1	2	—	0
3	60	1	3	3	—	—	0
4	04	0	—	3	—	—	0
5	46	1	4	4	—	—	0
6	31	0	—	4	—	—	0
7	67	1	5	5	—	—	0
8	25	0	—	5	—	—	0
9	24	0	—	—	—	—	0
10	10	0	—	—	—	—	0
11	40	1	6	6	—	—	0
12	02	0	—	6	—	—	0
13	39	0	—	—	—	—	0
14	68	1	7	7	—	—	0
15	08	0	—	7	—	—	0
16	59	1	8	8	—	—	0
17	66	1	9	8	9	—	0
18	90	2	10,11	10	9	11	1
19	12	0	—	10	11	—	0
20	64	1	12	12	11	—	0
21	79	2	13,14	12	13	14	1
22	31	0	—	14	13	—	0
23	86	2	15,16	14	15	16	1
24	68	1	17	16	15	17	1
25	82	2	18,19	16	17	18,19	2
26	89	2	20,21	18	17	19,20,21	3
27	80	2	22,23	18	19	20,21,22,23	4
28	11	0	—	20	19	21,22,23	3
29	62	1	24	20	21	22,23,24	3
30	16	0	—	22	21	23,24	2

5

FACILITY LOCATION

Description of the problem

A big controversy erupted in Carlisle, Pa., because the ABF Trucking Company wanted to build a new terminal that was to be the biggest in the nation. The residents of the area were fighting the new terminal because they felt that it would create too much air and noise pollution. This is an example of one problem that many businesses face when establishing a new location.

Many factors must be considered when a company opens a new store or plant. One of the most important considerations is where to locate the facility so that the distances traveled by suppliers and customers, or the distances its product must be shipped, are kept to a minimum. A company can save thousands of dollars every year by properly locating its facility, since the cost of shipping products today is so high.

Mathematics concepts required: Simple geometry and graphing

Appropriate for students in: Algebra 1

Specific problem

This type of problem requires geometry in its solution. To get an idea of the mathematics involved, we will consider a simpler type of problem in

29

which we decide where to locate a school-bus shelter for a group of seven students living along a road. Suppose one student lives in each house. The distances between their houses are given below. A school-bus-stop shelter is to be erected for the students to share while they wait for the bus. Determine where the shelter should be located so that the total distance the seven students have to walk is the minimum amount.

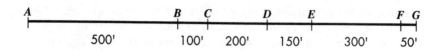

Model

Take a guess where the shelter should be located.

To determine the best location, we will begin by setting up a number line for the houses that will determine the location of each house by a coordinate on the number line rather than give the distances from each house to the shelter location.

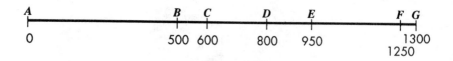

To make the problem easier, let us begin by using a limited number of the houses in the problem. If there were only one house, A, our number line would be

$$\frac{A}{0}$$

and we could determine the solution by setting up a table as follows:

Number of students	Shelter location	Total distance traveled
1	A	0

Thus, the answer would be to locate the shelter at house A.

Let us consider the first three houses in the problem and the midpoint of the segment, which seems like a good choice of location.

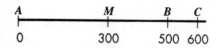

Setting up a table similar to the one above, we get the following:

Number of students	Shelter location	Total distance traveled
3	A	$BA + CA = 500 + 600 = 1100'$
	M	$AM + BM + CM =$
	B	$AB + CB =$
	C	$AC + BC =$

1. Complete the table and determine where the best location would be in this situation.

Let us consider what will happen if we use the first five houses and the midpoint of the segment.

Number of students	Shelter location	Total distance traveled
5	A	$BA + CA + DA + EA =$
	M	$AM + BM + CM + DM + EM =$
	B	
	C	
	D	
	E	

2. Finish the chart and determine where the best location would be. Do you see a pattern emerging?

Try the problem for all seven houses and a midpoint. Can you guess what the answer will be on the basis of the answers to the previous problem?

3. Complete the chart below and make sure your guess was correct.

Number of students	Shelter location	Total distance traveled
7	A	
	B	
	C	
	M	
	D	
	E	
	F	
	G	

Student assignment

1. In the model, the only location we tried to find for the shelter that was not at one of the houses was the midpoint between the first and last house. How can we be sure that there is not another shelter location that would reduce the total distance traveled? (Hint! A good way to show this answer is to draw a graph comparing the total distance traveled to the location of the shelter, as illustrated below for the situation with three houses.)

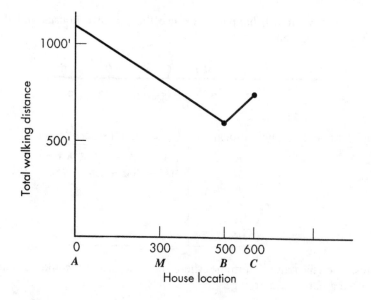

2. Formulate a general rule telling where to locate the shelter so that the total distance traveled is shortest when there is an odd number of houses.

3. Will the rule that you developed in problem 2 be true if the houses are located so that six of them are close together and the seventh one is far away, as illustrated below?

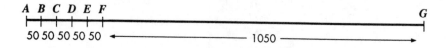

4. In the model, we considered what would happen with an odd number of houses. What would happen if there were an even number of houses

on the block? Suppose that six houses were located as illustrated below.

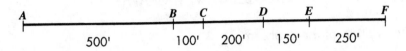

Repeat the procedures in the model for two, four, and six houses, then determine a rule that tells where to locate the shelter for an even number of houses.

6

TRAVELING WITH GRAPHS

Description of the problem

Carl has been studying the use of graphs in his algebra 1 class. The teacher said that speed/time graphs could be used as models to find the distances covered during a trip, but she did not explain how this could be done. Carl enjoys bike riding. He frequently takes long rides and has a speedometer on his bike. He decides to experiment, and during his next bike ride, he collects speed/time data for the trip. On returning home, he graphs it to see how he might find the distance he traveled.

© 1986 VOLK

Mathematics concepts required: Simple linear graphing; knowledge of the distance, time, rate formulas.

Appropriate for students in: Algebra 1

Model

Carl's bike trip takes 3.5 hours. During each hour of the trip, Carl notes the speed at which he is traveling. The trip is over level ground, and for most of the trip Carl maintains a constant speed, since he is a good rider. His data are as follows:

Hours	0	1	2	3	3.5
Speed (mph)	0	8	8	8	0

For these data, he plots a speed/time graph.

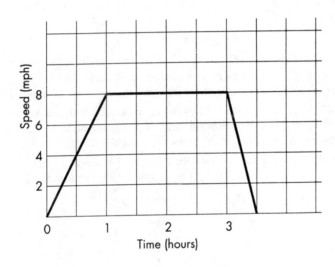

Carl knows the distance formula, $d = r \times t$, so for the two hours he traveled at 8 mph, he computes $8 \times 2 = 16$ miles. What does this have to do with the graph? Then he realizes that the area of the region of the graph between 1 and 3 hours, that is, the time when he maintained 8 mph, is equal to 16 square units. *Thus, the area under a speed/time graph represents distance.*

1. Use this principle to find the distances traveled during the first hour and last half hour.
2. According to the graph, what was Carl's speed at the end of thirty minutes?
3. What is the total distance covered during this trip?
4. During a five-hour bike ride, Carl again collects speed/time data and graphs it below. What is the total distance Carl traveled during this ride?

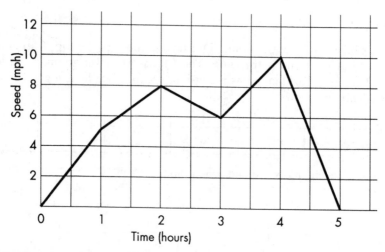

5. The time during which a body has a constant increase in velocity is called a period of acceleration, and the body is said to be accelerating. What are the periods of acceleration for the two trips discussed above?

6. A period during which a body has a constant decrease in velocity is called a period of deceleration, and the body is said to be decelerating. What are the periods of deceleration for the two trips?

7. Assume that during a period of time, t, a body accelerates in speed until it reaches a velocity, v. The graph of this situation is as follows:

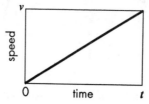

Write a formula in terms of t and v that will give the distance traveled during a time period.

Student assignment

1. When a body accelerates, it is said to have an acceleration, usually denoted by a where

$$a = \frac{\text{change in velocity}}{\text{change in time}}.$$

Consider the graph given in the last exercise above. What property of the line from $(0, 0)$ to (t, v) corresponds to acceleration?

2. Write an expression that relates acceleration to velocity and time.

3. Use the information obtained from the exercises above to find a formula for distance traveled during a period of constant acceleration.

4. A sprinter can cover 100 meters in about 10 seconds. Sketch a speed/time graph of how you think a 100-meter sprinter might run the course.

5. Assume you can run a 5-mile race in 25 minutes. The course is over level ground. Sketch a speed/time graph for your race. Assume that the same race is now cross-country. The course includes three hills: a small hill of gradual grade, a small hill with steep sides, and finally, a high hill with gradually sloping sides. You run this course in 30 minutes. Sketch a graph of your cross-country run.

6. A girl goes down a snow-covered hill on a sled. Her speed/time graph is as follows:

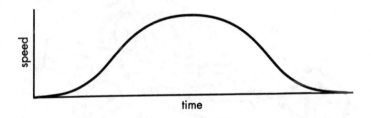

Describe her sled ride.

7

DELIVERING THE MAIL

Description of the problem

A letter carrier needs to deliver the mail to both sides of a street whose length is represented by L. She can deliver to all the boxes on one side, cross the street, and deliver to all the boxes on the other side. Or she can deliver to one box, cross the street, deliver to two boxes, cross again and deliver to two boxes, and so forth, until all the mail has been delivered. Which method is better?

MR. ZIP

Mathematics concepts required: Algebra (manipulating equations and inequalities)

Appropriate for students in: Algebra 1

Model

Assume there are n houses with a mailbox in the middle of each lot on each side of the street. Each side of the street is a mirror image of the other. W will represent the street width. The two paths for the letter carrier are diagramed in figure 7.1.

(*Comment*: The assumptions made are realistic for some streets and unrealistic for others. In any modeling project, it is helpful to start with simplified assumptions for analysis and then to gradually change the assumptions to represent more realistic situations.)

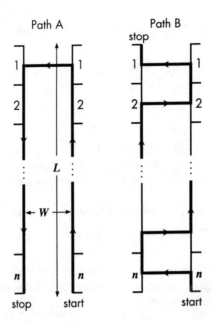

Fig. 7.1

Path A in figure 7.1 has length $2L + W - L/n$. L/n is subtracted to account for crossing at the mailbox for lot 1 instead of going to the end of the street. $(L/n)/2$, half of one lot width, is saved on each side of the street.

Path B has length $nW + L$.

The diagram assumes n is odd, but the length formula is also valid if n is even. By considering the special cases $n = 4, 5, 6$, and 7, you see that the number of times the street is crossed is equal to the number of houses on one side of the street.

If $2L + W - L/n = nW + L$, then the paths are equally good. The equation can be manipulated to find the implied relationship among W, L, and n:

$$2L - L - L/n = nW - W$$
$$L - L/n = (n - 1) W$$
$$L (1 - 1/n) = (n - 1) W$$
$$L/n (n - 1) = (n - 1)W$$

Therefore $$L/n = W.$$

This equation gives the *indifference relationship* between the parameters of a street. Since each of the steps above is reversible when $L/n = W$, the paths have the same length.

Now, suppose $nW + L < 2L + W - L/n$, that is, assume path B is shorter:

$$nW - W < 2L - L - L/n$$
$$(n - 1)\, W < L(1 - 1/n)$$
$$(n - 1)W < L/n\, (n - 1)$$
$$W < L/n$$

Since the steps are all reversible, $W < L/n$, that is, the street width is less than the lot width, implies that path B is shorter.

Similarly, it can be shown that $W > L/n$ implies that path A is shorter.

Suggestions for further study and potential extensions

1. Solve the problem if the mailboxes are not at the center of each lot. Assume all lots have the same width.
2. Solve the problem if the lot widths vary but each side of the street is a mirror image of the other. Assume that mailboxes are at the center of the front boundary of each lot.

8

THE GREENING OF FOREST ACRES

Description of the problem

A lawn-service contractor wishes to establish his business in the new Forest Acres housing development. All lot sizes are the same, and each property would require approximately the same maintenance services. The contractor estimates the cost of his services for each homeowner would be $275 a year. Forest Acres has 400 homes. He knows from past experience that in such a situation he can count on about 100 customers, but he would like more. In order to attract more clients, he advertises a special. For each "bonus customer" over 100, he will give a discount of $1.50 to all customers in the development. Under this policy, how many customers will provide the greatest revenue for the contractor?

Mathematics concepts required: Basic operations, knowledge of functions

Appropriate for students in: Algebra 1

Model

The lawn-service contractor's revenue is the total money received for his services. If 100, or fewer, customers sign up for the services, the contractor

41

will receive $275 from each one. For example, if 98 customers sign up, the contractor will receive revenues of $98 \times \$275 = \$26\ 950$.

If more than 100 customers enroll, *each* customer is entitled to a discount. Each annual bill will decrease by $1.50 per household for each customer over 100. The larger the number of customers, the cheaper the lawn service to everyone.

Using table 8.1 will help you understand the number-of-customers-to-cost relationship.

TABLE 8.1

Number of customers (C)	Charges to each customer ($)	Total revenues (R)
100	275	27 500
101	$275 - (1.50 \times 1)$	27 623.50
102	$275 - (1.50 \times 2)$	27 744
.	.	.
.	.	.
.	.	.
110	$275 - (1.50 \times 10)$	28 600
.	.	.
.	.	.
150	$275 - (1.50 \times 50)$	30 000
.	.	.
.	.	.
.	.	.
200	$275 - (1.50 \times 100)$	25 000

Do you see how the charges are reduced? With 102 customers, we have two bonus customers. These two bonus customers earn a $3 discount—$1.50 \times 2 = \$3.00$—for all 102 customers, reducing everyone's charges to $275 - (1.50 \times 2) = \$272$. Thus, with two extra customers, the total revenues received are $\$272 \times 102 = \$27\ 744$.

Use a calculator to find other entries for this table. Develop a search pattern to find the number of customers needed to obtain maximum revenues for the contractor.

1. What number of customers appears to yield the maximum revenue?
2. Check your result by trying one customer more and one customer less than your answer above.
3. Does this prove your answer?
4. Does this type of enrollment plan seem reasonable for a business to try? In his advertisement statement, how can the contractor protect himself so he doesn't lose money?
5. Write the relationship between the number of customers, C, and the total revenues, R, as a function.
6. Find the maximum amount of revenue if the discount is $1.75 for each enrollment over 120 customers.

9

JEEP IN THE DESERT

Description of the problem

A jeep can carry 50 gallons of fuel in its regular tank and in auxiliary cans attached to the chassis. The jeep can travel 10 miles on one gallon of fuel and needs to travel 1000 miles into a desert to rendezvous with a helicopter. Since the only supply of fuel is at the starting point, the jeep must prestock fuel along the proposed route. In order to get the jeep 1000 miles into the desert with a minimum amount of fuel, where along its route, and in what quantities, should the fuel be stockpiled?

| *Mathematics concepts required:* | Arithmetic, algebra |
| *Appropriate for students in:* | Algebra 1 |

Model

For a problem where a standard model does not seem to fit, a *heuristic* approach may be employed:

Stage 1—Without regard for minimizing the fuel used, find a stockpiling strategy that will get the job done.

Stage 2—Attempt to improve the solution found in the first stage. If possible, develop a systematic procedure for improving the first solution.

Stage 3—Determine whether the procedure developed in the second stage repeatedly yields a good solution. Is the result optimal? Are other solutions equally good?

In summary, this approach involves finding an initial solution and a procedure for repeatedly improving the solution until it appears that no further improvement is possible.

Solution

The objective is to move 50 gallons of fuel to the 500-mile marker. The remaining 500 miles can then be covered.

A diagram of the amount of fuel to be stockpiled and the location of each stockpile follows. The circled number represents the number of times the jeep leaves the previous supply point with a full (50 gallon) load of fuel.

Gallons of fuel stockpiled

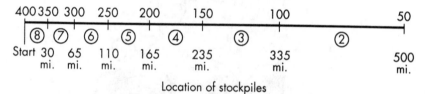

Location of stockpiles

Representative calculations and explanation:

In order to get 50 gallons of fuel to the 500-mile marker, it is necessary to make at least two trips from the previous supply point (since the maximum capacity is 50 gallons and some fuel will be used in the process of moving the fuel). The strategy is to use exactly two trips and to place the previous supply dump as far from the 500-mile mark as possible. If d_1 represents the distance from the supply point that precedes the 500-mile mark, then

$$\frac{3d_1}{10} + 50 = 100, \text{ so}$$

$$d_1 = \frac{500}{3} = 166\frac{2}{3} > 165.$$

100 represents two full loads of 50 gallons.

50 gallons is the amount needed at the 500-mile mark.

$\frac{3d_1}{10}$ is the number of gallons used for one round trip and the last one-way trip of d_1 miles.

By similar reasoning, at least three trips are required to get 100 gallons to the 335-mile marker. The relevant equation is $\frac{5d_2}{10} + 100 = 150$,

where d_2 represents the maximum distance from the 335-mile marker back to the previous supply dump.

150 = 3 trips × 50 gallons a trip

100 is the number of gallons needed at the 335-mile marker.

$\frac{5d_2}{10}$ is the number of gallons used for two round trips and used for the last one-way trip of d_2 miles.

$$\frac{5d_2}{100} = 50$$

$$d_2 = \frac{500}{5} = 100$$

The solution follows by repeating the procedure.

Note: If $\frac{500}{3}, \frac{500}{5}, \frac{500}{7}, \frac{500}{9}, \frac{500}{11}, \frac{500}{13}$, and $\frac{500}{15}$ are used to locate the supply dumps instead of 165, 100, 70, 55, 45, 35, and 30, the number of gallons can be reduced to 384.

10

MANAGING A DEER POPULATION

Description of the problem

In the early years of settlement on the east coast of the United States, the white-tailed deer roamed freely and was a source of food for the Indians and settlers. At this time, the deer population probably numbered in the hundreds of thousands. Gradually, as the region developed, the size of the deer herds diminished. With residential, agricultural, and industrial development, the deer's living range has been greatly reduced to the available forestlands. American white-tailed deer remain a natural resource whose beauty can be enjoyed in the wild. Deer hunting provides recreation for hunters every fall. The size of deer herds depends on a delicate balance. If the herds become too large, that is, if the number of deer exceed the amount of available food, deer starve and die. The starving deer destroy agricultural crops and cause traffic hazards through their wide migration patterns. Therefore, the size and quality of deer herds must be carefully monitored and controlled by wildlife officials. This control is accomplished by issuing hunting licenses and establishing special hunting seasons, for example, in doe seasons the female deer may also be hunted.

Dauphin County, Pennsylvania, in 1989 had an estimated deer population of 9399 animals, distributed as follows:

Adult males (bucks)	1707	Male fawns	2058
Adult females (does)	3714	Female fawns	1920

Develop a model to study the growth of Dauphin County's deer population over the next ten years.

Mathematics concepts required: Arithmetic

Appropriate for students in: Algebra 1

Model

Available game-commission statistics indicate the following:

1. Fawns are considered adults at two years of age.
2. Approximately 150 fawns are produced for every 100 does in the population. For every 100 female fawns, 107 male fawns are born.
3. Allowing for natural seasonal mortalities, 55 percent of all fawns born reach one year of age, and of these, 60 percent survive to two years of age. The natural survival rate for adults is 90 percent.

Elementary algebra can now be used to construct a mathematical model. Let M and F represent the current numbers of adult bucks and does, respectively. For 1989, $M = 1707$ and $F = 3714$. Without additional information on the age distribution of the fawns, assume two-thirds of the males and females are newborns. Represent these numbers by $M1$ and $F1$, respectively. Thus, $M1 = 2/3 \times 2058$ and $F1 = 2/3 \times 1920$. Assume the remaining fawns are one year of age and denote the numbers of these males and females by $M2$ and $F2$. At the beginning of the period one year from now, the deer population can be described as follows:

1.	New male fawns ($M1$):	$.52 * 1.5 * F$
2.	New female fawns ($F1$):	$.48 * 1.5 * F$
3.	One-year-old male fawns ($M2$):	$.55 * M1$
4.	One-year-old female fawns ($F2$):	$.55 * F1$
5.	Adult males (M):	$.90 * M + .6 * M2$
6.	Adult females (F):	$.90 * F + .6 * M2$

Thus, the total herd is $M + F + M1 + F1 + M2 + F2$. Use this information to complete the following chart:

Deer population distribution

Year	Herd size	Adult males	Adult females	Male fawns	Female fawns
1989	9399	1707	3714	2058	1920
1990					
1991					
1992					
.					
.					
.					
1999					

Student assignment

Now that we have a mathematical model for describing the deer population, write a computer program that uses the model to simulate changes in the herd size over the next ten years.

Recall that INT(X) computes the greatest integer less than or equal to X. Using the INT function, modify the program so that the values printed are rounded to the nearest integer.

Additional problems

1. Modify the program so the user can enter a hunting-season harvest size of 78 percent on adult males. Then investigate the effects of this annual harvest on the herd size over a ten-year period.

2. Change the program in exercise 2 so that it permits the annual harvesting of adult females (assume a 50 percent harvest rate on males and females), and examine the effects of this policy on herd size over a period of ten years.

11

GETTING THE WORD OUT

Description of the problem

A concert promoter is negotiating radio and television time for advertising an upcoming concert. She has up to $20 000 to spend on the promotion. Each twenty-second radio commercial costs $100, whereas thirty seconds of television time associated with major programming costs $800. She wants at least thirty radio spots distributed among various stations, but no more than sixty radio announcements in total. She would also like to have at least fifteen television commercials. How much radio time and TV time can she schedule to maximize advertising exposure and yet remain within the allotted budget?

| *Mathematics concepts required:* | Graphing inequalities, evaluating functions |
| *Appropriate for students in:* | Algebra 2 |

Model

To solve this problem, let *r* represent the number of radio spots and *t* the number of television spots. The expression for which a maximum value is desired is $20r + 30t$, representing the total number of seconds of air time. This will be called the *objective function*.

Both r and t are subject to several constraints described below and written in inequality form. The promoter wants

- at least thirty radio spots but no more than sixty ($30 \le r \le 60$);
- at least fifteen television spots ($t \ge 15$);
- to spend no more than $20 000 ($100r + 800t \le 20\ 000$).

Graph the intersection set of the three inequalities on an rt-coordinate plane. (See fig. 11.1.) The shaded region represents the set of points that satisfy the contraints. Within the region any point will supply a satisfactory answer for the objective function; however, an answer is needed that will satisfy and maximize the objective function under the given constraints. Such an answer will be given by an extreme point of the set, that is, a point that lies on the boundary of the set. In particular, the required answer will be found at one of the corners of the region. (Why?)

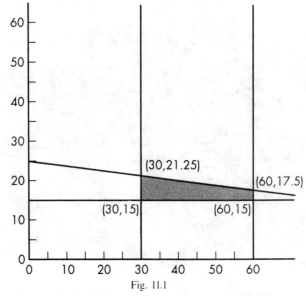

Fig. 11.1

To find the maximum value of $20r + 30t$ over the feasibility region, evaluate the expression at the four corners:

Point	$20r + 30t$
(30, 15)	1050
(30, 21.25)	1237.5
(60, 17.5)	1725
(60, 15)	1650

Note that the maximum value of the objective function occurs at (60, 17.5). The promoter should plan to schedule sixty radio spots and seventeen television spots.

Student assignment

Answer the following questions about the model:

1. What is the total advertising time for the derived solution?
2. How much will the advertising cost for the derived solution?
3. If the cost of a twenty-second radio ad is increased to $150, the other conditions remaining the same, how should the promoter purchase advertising time to maximize exposure?

12

AN IRRIGATION PROBLEM

Description of the problem

A linear irrigation system consists of a long water pipe on wheels with sprinklers mounted at regular intervals along the pipe. The system moves slowly across a rectangular field to give all parts of the field the same designated amount of water.

The manufacturer wants you to decide how to space the sprinkers on the pipe to give the *most uniform coverage* of water possible. After you have established the best spacing, you should decide how fast the system should move across the field to drop one inch of water in one pass.

Here are the specifications:

1. Each sprinkler head produces the spray pattern shown below. The flow rate is five gallons a minute for each sprinkler. That is, water falls uniformly on the area between two concentric circles with radii of one foot and twenty feet.

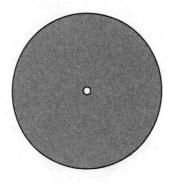

2. The field is 1000 feet wide and 2000 feet long.
3. To avoid runoff, there should be no more than double overlap of spray patterns.

Mathematics concepts required: Equation of circle

Appropriate for students in: Algebra 2

Model

To get uniform coverage, spray patterns must overlap. What would happen if the outer circles of the spray patterns were tangent?

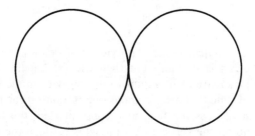

If the distance between the sprinklers is called d, you need to find the "best" value for d so that $20 \le d < 40$. ($d < 20$ results in at least triple overlap of spray patterns! Right?)

Here is a diagram for $20 < d < 40$:

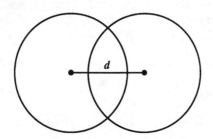

Put the circles on a rectangular coordinate system in a convenient way. Since the same behavior will occur all along the pipe, it is enough to look at only two spray patterns (fig. 12.1).

Now, we can write the equations for the three circles:

$$C_1: \quad x^2 + y^2 = 20^2$$
$$C_2: \quad (x - d)^2 + y^2 = 20^2$$
$$C_3: \quad x^2 + y^2 = 1^2$$

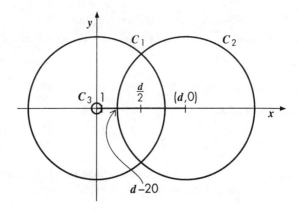

Fig. 12.1

Recall that your objective is to provide uniform water coverage. This objective must be translated into a mathematical statement. The amount of water placed on a square inch of land x units away from the y-axis depends on the amount of time that area is under one or more spray patterns. Since the system moves across the field at a constant rate, the time under the spray will depend on the vertical chord lengths through the square inch of land. For some values of x there will be one chord, and for others there will be two.

Complete uniformity would require that the sum of the vertical chord lengths through x be the same for all x. Since this is not possible, the most uniform coverage will then be obtained by selecting d so that the difference between the maximum- and minimum-chord sums is as small as possible.

Let's call $C(x)$ the "sum of vertical chords" function.

$$C(x) = \begin{cases} 2\left(\sqrt{400 - x^2} - \sqrt{1 - x^2}\right) & \text{for } 0 \le x \le 1 \\ 2\sqrt{400 - x^2} & \text{for } 1 < x \le d - 20 \\ 2\left[\sqrt{400 - x^2} + \sqrt{400 - (x - d)^2}\right] & \text{for } d - 20 < x \le d/2 \end{cases}$$

The graph of $C(x)$ will look like that shown in figure 12.2. You should graph $C(x)$ for at least one value of d by plotting points, using a computer, or using calculus. From the graph, it is clear that the largest value of $C(x)$ occurs at 1 or $d/2$, and the smallest at $d - 20$.

The problem can be solved by completing table 12.1 and selecting the d value that yields the smallest entry in the last column.

1. How far apart should the sprinklers be?
2. How many sprinklers are needed?

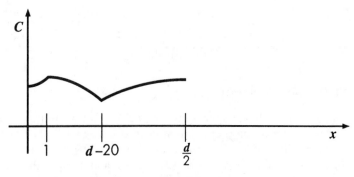

Fig. 12.2

3. Where should the end unit be placed?
4. How fast, in feet per hour, should the device move across the field so that the *average* waterfall is one inch?
5. What is the most water any portion of land will receive?
6. What is the least?

TABLE 12.1

d	$C(1)$	$C(d/2)$	$C(d - 20)$	$C_{Max} - C_{Min}$
21				
22				
23				
24				
25				
26				
27				
28				
29				
30				
31				
32				
33				
34				
35				
36				
37				
38				
39				

Suggestions for further study

Solve the problem if triple overlap of spray patterns is permitted. Does this solution give more uniform coverage?

13

PAPER ROLLS

Description of the problem

Many materials, such as paper, steel, plastic, and aluminum, are placed on rolls for shipment to another location for processing. A typical problem is finding the number of feet of paper stored on a roll with an outer radius of 5.75 inches and an inner radius of 1.75 inches, and a paper thickness of 0.003 inches. The inner radius is the core around which the paper is wrapped. If the paper is being unwrapped at a constant rate of 10 feet a minute, then the time remaining until the paper supply is exhausted is also of interest.

Mathematics concepts required: Arithmetic series

Appropriate for students in: Algebra 2

Model

Since the circumference of a circle is given by $C = 2\pi r$, the first wrap of paper around the core has a length of $2\pi(1.75)$ inches. The second wrap goes over one layer of paper, so that its length is $2\pi(1.75 + 0.003)$ inches. The third wrap goes over two layers and has a length of $2\pi[1.75 + (2)(0.003)]$. The total length L of the paper on the roll is therefore approximately (why not exactly?)

$$2\pi(1.75) + 2\pi[1.75 + (1)(0.003)]$$
$$+ 2\pi[1.75 + 2(0.003)] + \ldots + 2\pi[1.75 + (N-1)(0.003)]$$

inches, where N is the number of wraps around the core. Note that

$$N = \frac{5.75 - 1.75}{0.003} \simeq 1333,$$

if the paper is wrapped tightly.

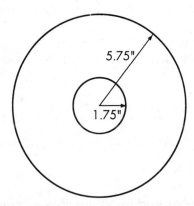

To find the number of feet of paper on the roll, we note that L can be written

$$2\pi(1.75) + 2\pi[1.75 + 0.003] + 2\pi[1.75 + 2(0.003)]$$
$$+ \ldots + 2\pi[1.75 + 1332(0.003)]$$
$$= 2\pi(1.75)(1333) + 2\pi[0.003 + 2(0.003) + \ldots + 1332(0.003)].$$

The sum $0.003 + 2(0.003) + \ldots + 1332(0.003)$ is a special case of the finite arithmetic series $a + 2a + \ldots + ka$.

To find a simple formula for the sum of the finite arithmetic series, let $S = a + 2a + \ldots + ka$, which can be written in reverse order as $S = ka + (k-1)a + \ldots + 1a$. By adding these expressions, we get

$$2S = (k+1)a + (k+1)a + \ldots + (k+1)a \ (k \text{ times})$$
$$2S = k[(k+1)(a)]$$
$$S = \frac{k(k+1)a}{2}.$$

Using this formula for S, we find that L is therefore

$$1333\ (2\pi)(1.75)\ +\ 2\pi\ \frac{[(1332)(1333)(0.0037)]}{2}$$

$$\approx 14\ 657.1\ +\ 16\ 734.2\ \text{inches}$$
$$\approx 2616\ \text{feet.}$$

Since the paper is being unwrapped at 10 feet a minute, the number of minutes remaining until the paper is exhausted is $2616/10 = 261.6$ minutes, or about 4.36 hours.

Alternative solution

Calculate the area of the edge of the paper in two steps:

1. Area $= L\ (0.003)$, since the edge is a thin rectangle when the paper is stretched out.
2. Area $= \pi(5.75)^2 - \pi\ (1.75)^2$, since the edge area is between concentric circles with radii 5.75 inches and 1.75 inches.

Therefore

$$L = \frac{\pi\ (5.75)^2 - \pi\ (1.75)^2}{0.003} \approx 31\ 415.9\ \text{inches}$$
$$\approx 2\ 618\ \text{feet.}$$

The answers compare favorably.

Suggestions for further study and possible extensions

The problem described and solved previously is a special case of the general problem:

Find L (paper length) and T (time remaining until the paper supply is exhausted) as functions of r = inner radius of the roll in inches.

R = outer radius of the roll in inches

t = paper thickness in inches

F = rate at which the paper is unwrapped in feet per minute

Solution 1

N = number of wraps of paper $\approx [(R) - r)/t]$, where $[x]$ represents the greatest integer $\leq x$.

$$L = 2\pi rN + \frac{2\pi(N - 1)(N)t}{2}$$

$T = (L/12)/F$. Note that L is a quadratic function of N.

Solution 2

$$tL = \pi R^2 - \pi r^2$$

$$L = \frac{\pi R^2 - \pi r^2}{t}$$

$$T = (L/12)/F$$

For students who conquer the paper-roll problem, the related problem given below will provide an additional challenge.

A spool for storing 2-inch diameter cable has the dimensions shown in figures 13.1 and 13.2 below. Cable can be placed on the spool by stacking each strand directly above another (as shown in fig. 13.3) or by placing each strand directly between two strands of the previous layer (as shown in fig. 13.4).

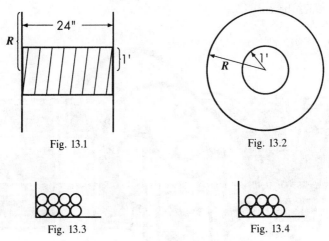

Fig. 13.1   Fig. 13.2

Fig. 13.3   Fig. 13.4

Find the best values of the outer radius R for each stacking method, when the objective is to store the largest number of linear feet of cable.

14

WHEN FOUR EQUALS THREE EQUALS TWO

Description of the problem

Congratulations! You have just been elected one of the sophomore delegates to the student council. The council has nine delegates—four seniors, three juniors, and two sophomores. You have been told that the seniors were given more votes so that they would have more power; the juniors were given fewer votes than the seniors so that they would have less power than the seniors; and the sophomores were given the least number of votes so that they would have the least amount of power of the three classes. But is that really the case?

Mathematics concepts required: Counting techniques, permutations

Appropriate for students in: General mathematics

Model

Game theory offers very interesting possibilities for the analysis of the voting power of individuals and the corresponding power of groups of voters, called blocs. Until recently, people believed that the number of votes a player controlled was directly proportional to his voting power. Therefore, a person with 50 percent of the votes should possess 50 percent of the power. For years, student councils have been constructed using this idea so that the seniors would have more power than the juniors, and the juniors more than the sophomores. A typical student council might consist of nine members—four seniors, three juniors, and two sophomores. It would appear that the seniors do possess more power; however, is that really true?

L. S. Shapley and Martin Shubik are two men prominent in the field of voting power. They developed a method for expressing the voting power for *groups* of voters, such as the seniors, and also the power for individuals within a group. The Shapley-Shubik method explains that the student council is the same as the game [5; 4,3,2]. The first number, 5, is called the *quota* and represents the number of votes necessary to pass an issue, or to win. Since there are nine members on the student council, the simple-majority rule would tell us that five votes is the minimum number necessary to win. The other numbers—4, 3, 2—represent the number of voters in each group. Thus, the first number, 4, represents four seniors, the 3 represents the three juniors, and the 2 represents the two sophomores.

To find the Shapley-Shubik Index, denoted I, first form all the permutations of the three classes. There are $3! = 3 \times 2 \times 1 = 6$ different ways to *order* the three classes. (In general, the number of permutations of n groups is $n!$.) Complete the table on the left below by filling in the missing class in each permutation.

Group orderings			*Sum of votes needed for majority*
1. Sr.	Jr.	So.	$4 + 3 = 7 \geq 5$
2. Sr.	So.	—	
3. Jr.	—	So.	
4. —	So.	Sr.	
5. So.	—	Jr.	
6. —	Jr.	Sr.	

Next, add the number of votes each class casts until the sum equals or exceeds 5. Circle the class that was the last one added that changed the vote from losing to winning. This class is called *pivotal*. In the first case, the seniors would cast their four votes, but that would not be enough to win. The juniors would then cast their three votes, giving us a sum of $4 + 3 = 7$, and they would become the pivotal class in the first permutation. So circle *Jr.* Complete the rest of the table.

Finally, to find the I_{Game} for each class, count the number of times a class is pivotal (circled) and divide by the number of permutations. Thus $I_{Sr.} = I_{Jr.} = I_{So.} = 2/6 = 1/3$.

Therefore, the Shapley-Shubik Index for the game [5; 4,3,2] is $I = (1/3, 1/3, 1/3)$. Furthermore, since each senior must share his or her 1/3 of the power, the voting power of each individual can be calculated in the following way:

Senior: $\frac{1}{4} \times \frac{1}{3} = \frac{1}{12}$
Junior: $\frac{1}{3} \times \frac{1}{3} = $ _____
Sophomore: $\frac{1}{2} \times \frac{1}{3} = $ _____

and the $I_{\text{Individual}} = I_{\text{Game}}/\text{Number in the group} = (\frac{1}{12}, \frac{1}{12}, \frac{1}{12}, \frac{1}{12}, \frac{1}{9}, \frac{1}{9}, \frac{1}{9}, \frac{1}{6}, \frac{1}{6})$.

As one can see, the seniors do *not* possess more power. Rather, all three classes possess the same power because no *one* class can win, but any *two* classes can. Furthermore, when one examines the voting power of the individual students, *the sophomores*—not the seniors—possess the most power. The S-S Index assumes that all members of a group must vote together and that all combinations of groups are equally likely.

Consider another example. Two friends, Jim and Tim, each own a company. Both companies are managed by a board of directors composed of seven members—the owner and an equal number of representatives from each division in the company. Jim's Junk Company has two divisions—collection (COLL) and distribution (DIST); therefore, each division has three representatives on the board. Tim's Toy Company has three divisions—manufacturing (MAN), advertising (ADV), and sales (SAL). Each division in Tim's Company has two delegates to the board. The composition of the two boards can be summarized as follows:

Jim's Junk Company

Division	Number of board members
Collection (COLL)	3
Distribution (DIST)	3
Owner (JIM)	1
Total	7

Tim's Toy Company

Division	Number of board members
Manufacturing (MAN)	2
Advertising (ADV)	2
Sales (SAL)	2
Owner (TIM)	1
Total	7

As long as the board members vote independently, they will each possess $\frac{1}{7}$ of the voting power. However, it has been noted that the several divisions tend to band together and vote as a group. As a result, the board of Jim's Junk Company would be the same as the game [4; 3 (COLL), 3 (DIST), 1 (JIM)]. Similarly, the board of Tim's Toy Company would be the same as the game [4; 2 (MAN), 2 (ADV), 2 (SAL), 1 (TIM)]. If the divisions vote as groups, do you think that Jim and Tim will have an equal amount of power on their respective boards?

First, look at the game for Jim's company, [4; 3,3,1]. Do you see any similarity between this game and the game for the student council, [5; 4,3,2]? _____ Although the numbers are different, in both cases we find that no one group can pass an issue, but *any* two can. Do you think that the Shapley-Shubik Index for both games will be the same? Let's see. Begin by forming the 3! = 6 permutations of the three groups—collection (COLL), distribution (DIST), and owner (JIM). Then, add the votes until you reach or exceed the quota. Circle the name of the last group whose votes were necessary to reach the quota. Complete the table below.

Group orderings

1. COLL DIST JIM $3 + 3 = 6 \geq 4$, so we circle DIST
2. COLL JIM   DIST $3 + 1 = 4 \geq 4$, so we circle JIM
3. DIST COLL JIM
4. DIST JIM   COLL
5. JIM   COLL DIST
6. JIM   DIST COLL

Thus, each group is pivotal two out of the six times, which implies $I_{JIM} = (\frac{2}{6}, \frac{2}{6}, \frac{2}{6}) = (\frac{1}{3}, \frac{1}{3}, \frac{1}{3})$. If you guessed that the games for the student council and Jim's company would yield the same result, you were right!

Now let us look at the game for Tim's Toy Company, [4; 2,2,2,1]. This time we have four different groups—manufacturing (MAN), advertising (ADV), sales (SAL), and owner (TIM). As a result, we will have 4! = $4 \times 3 \times 2 \times 1 = 24$ permutations of the groups. Can you complete the following table by supplying the missing group? (Remember, each group appears exactly once in each ordering.)

Group orderings

MAN	ADV	SAL	TIM	ADV	MAN	SAL	TIM
MAN	ADV	TIM	___	ADV	MAN	___	SAL
MAN	___	ADV	TIM	ADV	___	MAN	TIM
MAN	SAL	TIM	ADV	ADV	SAL	TIM	MAN
MAN	TIM	___	SAL	___	TIM	MAN	SAL
___	TIM	SAL	ADV	ADV	TIM	SAL	___

SAL	MAN	ADV	TIM		TIM	___	ADV	SAL
SAL	___	TIM	ADV		TIM	MAN	SAL	ADV
SAL	ADV	MAN	___		___	ADV	MAN	SAL
SAL	ADV	TIM	MAN		TIM	ADV	___	MAN
SAL	TIM	___	ADV		TIM	SAL	MAN	ADV
___	TIM	ADV	MAN		TIM	SAL	ADV	___

Next, for each permutation, add the votes for each group until the quota is reached. Circle the pivotal group. How many times has Manufacturing been pivotal? ___ Advertising? ___ Sales? ___ Tim? ___ Now divide each number by the total number of permutations—24—to get the Shapley-Shubik Index. Therefore, the $I_{TIM} = (\frac{8}{24}, \frac{8}{24}, \frac{8}{24}, 0) = (\frac{1}{3}, \frac{1}{3}, \frac{1}{3}, 0)$.

Our results indicate that although each owner casts one of the seven votes on his respective board, Jim possesses $\frac{1}{3}$ of the voting power for his company, but Tim is just a figurehead with *no* power at all.

Additional ideas to think about

1. Determine the I-value for the following games:

   (a) [5; 4, 4, 1]
   (b) [25; 24, 21, 4]

Banzhaf, a second method for calculating voting power, examines the outcomes—rather than the order—of the voting. In general, there are 2^n possible yes or no outcomes for n voters. In the student council game, for example, we have $2^3 = 8$ (3 classes) possible outcomes. See the first three columns in table 14.1.

We count the total number of yes votes to determine whether the issue would pass (votes that equal or exceed the quota) or would fail. Examine each outcome. If the issue passed, we then look at each group that voted yes. If any *one group at a time* were to change to a no vote, would the issue then fail? If it would, circle that group, and continue to check all the groups for each outcome. (*Note:* More than one group or no group may be circled on one line.) Similarly, if the issue fails, then we check each group that voted no. If any one of these groups changes to a yes vote, will the issue then pass? If it will, circle the group.

For example, when all three classes vote yes, the issue passes with nine votes. If any *one* class changes its votes to no, the issue will still pass; therefore, no class is pivotal. In the second example, the seniors and juniors voted yes for a total of seven votes, so the issue passes. However, if either group changes to a no vote, the issue will fail. As a result, each group—the seniors and the juniors—is pivotal and should be circled. The completed table should be as in table 14.2.

TABLE 14.1

	SR(4)	JR(3)	SO(2)	Total Votes	Result
1.	Yes	Yes	Yes	9	Pass
2.	Yes	Yes	No	7	Pass
3.	Yes	No	Yes	6	Pass
4.	No	Yes	Yes	5	Pass
5.	Yes	No	No	4	Fail
6.	No	Yes	No	3	Fail
7.	No	No	Yes	2	Fail
8.	No	No	No	0	Fail

TABLE 14.2

SR(4)	JR(3)	SO(2)
Yes	Yes	Yes
Yes	Yes	No
Yes	No	Yes
No	Yes	Yes
Yes	No	No
No	Yes	No
No	No	Yes
No	No	No

Thus, the Banzhaf Index, I, for the student council game is $I = (\frac{4}{12}, \frac{4}{12}, \frac{4}{12}) = (\frac{1}{3}, \frac{1}{3}, \frac{1}{3})$.

2. Calculate the Banzhaf Index for Jim's Junk and Tim's Toys. Is it the same as the Shapley-Shubik Index? _____ If it is, do you think they are always equal? _____

15

TIME TO WASTE

Description of the problem

The United States is the largest garbage producer in the world. Most of our garbage is dumped into the ground, often causing ground-water contamination and other pollution problems. In the next five years, over half of the nation's landfills will be full, leaving approximately 100 million people with nowhere to dispose of their garbage. Because of this dilemma, many cities are looking at alternatives. In addition, the cost of garbage disposal is rising at an alarming rate. In the last ten years, the cost of disposing garbage in landfills has gone up 300–400 percent in many areas. Philadelphia must send much of its waste as far away as Ohio. Disposing of waste is the number one expense for Saint Paul, Minnesota. In order to make adequate and financially feasible plans for the future, city and county planners need a way to predict the amount of garbage that will need placement.

BROOM HILDA

Reprinted by permission: Tribune Media Services.

Mathematics concepts required: Equation of straight line (point-slope formula), equation of parabola.

Appropriate for students in: Algebra 2

Specific problem

York County currently deposits over 99 percent of its waste in two county landfills. It is estimated that one of the two will be filled to capacity by 1990. Under the conditions of its lease, the second landfill must be closed by 1994. In order to plan for alternative means of waste disposal, the planning commission must know the approximate amount of garbage that will be produced in the future. Predict the amount of garbage that will be produced daily by York County in 1994.

Model

The first thing needed to solve this problem is data on garbage production in York County. (Unfortunately, no data were collected before 1970 when York County conducted its first study on the amount of garbage being produced. Before 1985, no scales were in use at the landfills, so the numbers given for 1970, 1975, and 1980 are estimates.)

Year	Garbage produced per day (in tons)
1970	453
1975	506.9
1980	598.8
1985	755

The next step of the solution is to plot the data provided. Using the graph in figure 15.1, plot the data from the last column above. Try to connect the points with a smooth curve or straight line.

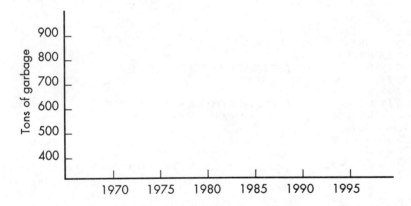

Fig. 15.1. Garbage produced per day

In order to make predictions, we must have some idea of what will happen to the graph in the future. One way to do this is by linear regression. Linear regression involves trying to find a straight-line equation that best fits the data—the straight line that most closely approximates the graph. Try to find the straight-line approximation that comes closest to all the plotted points. Using the point-slope formula, write the equation for your line. (*Hint:* Find two points on the straight-line approximation.)

Point-slope formula: $y - y_1 = m(x - x_1)$

Your equation: _____

A mathematical algorithm exists for determining the slope and y-intercept of the best straight-line approximation to the data. The algorithm can be implemented by hand, but because of time considerations, it is preferable to use a computer program (see, for example, fig. 15.2) or to use a scientific calculator.

```
100 PRINT "          LINEAR REGRESSION "
110 PRINT
120 PRINT "NUMBER OF KNOWN POINTS (0 OR LESS THAN ZERO TO QUIT) ";
130 INPUT N
140 IF N <= 0 THEN 700
150 DIM X(N), Y(N), Z(N)
160 REM - INITIALIZE VARIABLES
170 GOSUB 520
180 REM - READ DATA POINTS
190 GOSUB 460
200 REM - ACCUMULATE INTERMEDIATE SUMS
210 GOSUB 380
220 REM - COMPUTE CURVE COEFFICIENTS
230 GOSUB 540
240 A1 = A : B1 = B
250 FOR I = 1 TO N
260    X(I) = Z(I) * Z(I)
270 NEXT I
280 GOSUB 520
290 GOSUB 380
300 GOSUB 540
310 PRINT
320 PRINT "          LEAST SQUARE FOR ( A + B * X ) IS "
330 PRINT "F(X) = "; A1; " + (";B1; "* X)"
340 PRINT
350 PRINT "          LEAST SQUARE FOR ( A + B * X ^ 2) IS "
360 PRINT "G(X) = "; A; "+ ("; B; " * X)"
370 GOSUB 570
380 FOR I = 1 TO N
390    J = J + X(I)
400    K = K + Y(I)
410    L = L + X(I) * X(I)
420    M = M + Y(I) * Y(I)
430    R2 = R2 + X(I) * Y(I)
440 NEXT I
450 RETURN
460 FOR I = 1 TO N
470    PRINT "X, Y OF POINT "; I;
480    INPUT X(I), Y(I)
490    Z(I) = X(I)
500 NEXT I
510 RETURN
520 J = 0 : K = 0 : L = 0 : M = 0 : R2 = 0
530 RETURN
540 B = (N *R2 - K *J) / (N * L - J * J)
550 A = (K - B * J) / N
```

```
560 RETURN
570 PRINT
580 PRINT "INTERPOLATION (ENTER 0 TO END) "
590 PRINT "YEAR IS ";
600 INPUT T
610 IF T = 0 THEN 700
620 PRINT
630 PRINT "          USING ( A + B * X) "
640 PRINT "TONS PER DAY IS "; A1 + B1 * T
660 PRINT "          USING ( A + B * X ^ 2) "
670 PRINT "TONS PER DAY IS "; A + B * T
690 GOTO 570
700 END
```

Fig. 15.2

Enter the given data in the BASIC program shown in figure 15.2 and run the program. The independent variable X represents the year, and the dependent variable Y represents the daily production of garbage in tons for that year. Write the resulting equation:

Equation: _____

Compare this equation with the one that you worked out earlier. The computer-generated equation can now be used to predict the amount of garbage that will be produced in a day for any year in the near future. Predict the amount of garbage produced for 1987: _____ tons a day. (In July 1987, the average amount of garbage was 771 tons a day.) How accurate is your estimate?

Now predict the amount for 1994: _____ a day.

Suggestions for further study

Examining the graph of the given data indicates that a *parabola* may fit the data better. The computer program in figure 15.2 also finds and prints out the best parabolic fit of the form $Y = a + bX^2$.

Predict the 1987 and 1994 rates of garbage production using the best parabola.

To determine whether the straight line or the parabola fits the data better, complete the table below. The option for which the sum of the squares of the differences between the predicted and actual Y values is smaller is considered better.

X	Y	$a + bX$	$(a + bX) - Y$	$a + bX^2$	$(a + bX^2) - Y$
1970	453				
1975	506.9				
1980	598.8				
1985	755				

Sum of squares of column 4 entries = _____.
Sum of squares of column 6 entries = _____.
Therefore, the better fit is provided by _____.

Student assignment

1. The plans for York County waste disposal include building an incinerator that will be able to handle the garbage for the entire county. Approximately 15 percent of the waste is bottles and cans. It is hoped that the public can be convinced to recycle these products. Acknowledging the fact that bottles and cans will not burn, what must the capacity of the incinerator be for the year 1994?

2. The proposed incinerator has a burning capacity of 900 tons a day. According to your predictions, will this incinerator be able to handle the garbage needs of the county in the year 2000? Again, assume that cans and bottles are not burned.

3. Approximately 36 percent of the solid waste in York County is paper products. Another 40 percent of the waste is food products and other organic waste. These can be easily and economically recycled. If public awareness could be raised, the population convinced to sort their garbage, and recycling facilities made available, how many tons of garbage a day would have to be recycled in the year 1994? Assume that bottles and cans are already being recycled.

4. The Harrisburg Steam Generating Facility is willing to accept 200 tons of York County garbage each day. What percentage of the 1994 garbage could be disposed of in this manner?

5. At the current growth rate of garbage and population, how much garbage will be generated per person per day by the year 2000? (*Hint*: Use the program in figure 15.2 to make a prediction about the population of York County in the year 2000.)

6. The average amount of garbage produced per person in the United States in 1985 was 3.9 pounds per day. How does York County compare with this figure?

16

STREET PARKING

Description of the problem

You are on the planning commission for Algebraville, and plans are being made for the downtown shopping district revitalization. The streets are 60 feet wide, and an allowance must be made for both on-street parking and two-way traffic. Fifteen feet of roadway is needed for each lane of traffic. Parking spaces are to be 16 feet long and 10 feet wide, including the lines. Your job is to determine which method of parking—parallel or angle—will allow the most room for the parking of cars and still allow a two-way traffic flow.

Mathematics concepts required: Geometry, right triangle trigonometry

Appropriate for students in: Algebra 2

Model

We will design parking for one city block (0.1 mile) and use that design for the entire shopping district.

71

1. How many cars can be parked along one side of the street using parallel parking?

2. If parking is permitted on both sides of the street, how much roadway is left for traffic? Does this fit the specifications given above?

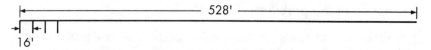

For angle parking, consider the diagram below, where ϕ is the angle the lines make with the curbing, c is the curb space required for the angle ϕ, and 10 is the required width of the space.

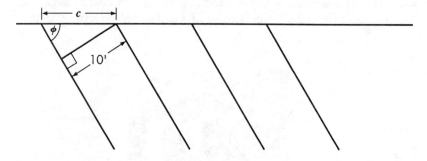

We must find a relationship among c, 10, and ϕ. Since the triangle is a right triangle, we can use the relationship $\sin \phi = 10/c$.

3. Solve the equation for c.

To determine the number of cars that can be parked on a side, experiment with various values of ϕ.

4. Copy and complete the table below. Round c to the nearest tenth, and round the cars/side down to the greatest integer less than or equal to the quotient of $528/c$.

ϕ	c	Cars/side
10		
15		
20		
25		
30		
45		
60		
75		
90		

5. Which angle allows for the greatest number of parked cars? Why is this an impractical angle to consider?

Next, we must determine the street width used for each angle. The diagram below should help find this information.

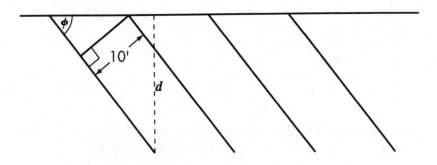

The desired relationship here is $\tan \phi = 10/x$.

6. Solve the equation for x.
7. According to the diagram, what is the length of each space?

Since we need to determine d, we will use the trigonometric ratio $\sin \phi = d/(x + 16)$.

8. Solve this equation for d.
9. Copy and complete the table below to find the street width needed for the parking spaces.

ϕ	x	d
10		
15		
20		
25		
30		
45		
60		
75		
90		

Since allowance is to be made for parking on both sides of the street, the amount of street width used for parking will be $2d$.

10. Copy and complete the table below to show the street width remaining for traffic.

ϕ	Street for driving
10	
15	
20	
25	
30	
45	
60	
75	
90	

You now have all the facts and figures and should be ready to present a proposal to the other members of the planning commission.

11. What is your recommendation, and why?

17

YELLOW TRAFFIC LIGHTS

Description of the problem

When a traffic light is installed, planning must include the duration of the green and the yellow lights. The correct duration of the green light limits the traffic congestion, enhances the traffic flow, and decreases pollution. The correct duration of the yellow light promotes safety by insuring proper stopping time. How is the duration of the yellow light determined?

Mathematics concepts required: Velocity, acceleration

Appropriate for students in: Algebra 2 or precalculus

Specific problem

Find a minimum safe duration for a yellow light in an 80-ft intersection. The intersection lies in a 45-mph speed zone.

Model

General information needed for the solution. To determine the proper duration of a yellow light, find the length of time needed to go through the intersection when it is not possible to stop safely. This leads to the question, When is it possible to stop safely? To answer this question, we will assume that the brakes are applied steadily and function properly throughout the stop.

Two equations from physics will be needed to solve this problem:

$$\text{Equation 1:} \quad x = v_0 t + at^2/2$$

$$\text{Equation 2:} \quad v^2 = v_0^2 + 2ax$$

x = distance
a = acceleration
v = velocity
t = time
v_0 = initial velocity

In addition, the velocity needs to be changed from 45 miles per hour to 66 feet per second.

The total stopping distance is composed of two parts:

1. Distance traveled during the time that the driver is reacting to the yellow light (x_r)
2. Distance traveled while the brakes are applied (x_b)

Distance traveled during reaction time. While the driver is reacting to the light, velocity remains constant, which means acceleration is 0. The reaction time may vary from 0.3 seconds to 1 second but averages 0.6 seconds. Using the equation

$$x_r = v_0 t_r \qquad (t_r = \text{reaction time}), \tag{1}$$

find the distance traveled for the average reaction time,

$$x_r = 66 \,(0.6) = 39.6 \text{ feet.}$$

Distance traveled while braking. When the driver is braking, acceleration takes on a negative value. Research indicates that the value varies considerably, depending on the car, the tires, the brakes, and the road conditions. Under excellent conditions, some cars may achieve an acceleration of -28.8 feet per second squared when braking (also called deceleration). Under very poor conditions such as icy roads, acceleration may be as poor as -12.8 feet per second squared. A typical deceleration is -19.2 feet per second squared. At an acceleration of -19.2 feet per second squared, a car traveling at 66 feet per second will be traveling at 46.8 feet per second one second after the brakes are applied.

To find the actual braking time, we will use the equation

$$v^2 = v_0^2 + 2ax_b. \tag{2}$$

Setting $v = 0$, we see that the equation for actual braking time becomes

$$x_b = -v_0^2/2a,$$

and $v_0 = 66$ ft/s, $a = -19.2$ ft/s^2, and $x_b = 4356/38.4 = 113.44$ ft.

Total braking distance. As previously noted, total braking distance is the distance traveled while reacting plus the distance traveled while braking,

$$39.6 \text{ ft} + 113.44 \text{ ft} = 153.04 \text{ ft}.$$

This means that under typical conditions a driver traveling 45 miles an hour will require approximately 153 feet to stop the car.

Time needed to travel through the intersection. For traffic to be controlled properly, the yellow light must have a duration that will allow a car to either stop completely before reaching the intersection or travel safely through the intersection. As shown in the computations above, a car traveling at 45 miles an hour less than 153 feet from the intersection when the light turns yellow should not try to stop but should proceed through the intersection. The total maximum distance a car must travel through the intersection is the width of the intersection plus the distance from the intersection. The maximum distance for our problem is

$$153 \text{ ft} + 80 \text{ ft} = 233 \text{ ft}.$$

Equation 1 will be used to find the travel time required for this distance. Because the driver is expected to travel through the intersection at a constant speed, acceleration will be set at 0. This yields the equation

$$t = x/v,$$
$$t = 233/66 = 3.53 \text{ sec}.$$

Duration of the yellow light. From the computations above, the minimum duration for the yellow light should be 3.5 seconds. To make a more informed decision, we will compute the maximum time required to travel through the intersection under poor conditions.

   a. If reaction time is 1 second, the distance traveled is 66 feet.

   b. If acceleration is -6.4 feet per second squared, the braking distance is 340.3 feet.

   c. The total distance becomes 486.3 feet.

   d. The time required to travel through the intersection is 7.4 seconds.

In the situation we have considered, the duration of a yellow traffic light at an 80-foot-wide intersection in a 45-mph speed zone should be between 3.5 and 7.4 seconds. The high value represents the time needed by a person with a high reaction time of one second. However, research shows that the majority of drivers with such delayed reactions are elderly and drive slower, usually below the speed limit. Furthermore, studies show that such drivers would probably drive at 35 miles per hour in a 45-mph speed zone. If this is assumed, then the yellow-light duration needed by these drivers would be 3.66 seconds. Thus, in a practical situation, it would seem that a period slightly more than 3.5 seconds would be an adequate duration for a yellow light. A time of 4 to 4.5 seconds would be a good choice.

It should be mentioned that if one is traveling above or below the speed limit, it is possible to be in a position where it is possible neither to stop safely nor to clear the intersection without accelerating.

Student assignment

1. How is 45 miles an hour changed to 66 feet per second?
2. Time the duration of a yellow traffic light near your home.
3. If a vehicle is traveling 70 miles an hour on the Kentucky Turnpike and is 200 feet behind the car in front of it, would it be able to stop in time to avoid a rear-end collision if the car in the front came to an abrupt stop? Assume $t = 0.3$ second and $a = -15$ feet per second.
4. Find x when $a = -24$ feet per second if the car is traveling at
   a. 20 mph;
   b. 60 mph.
5. A large truck is traveling on an icy road. The speed limit on the road is 50 miles an hour. If the truck is traveling at the speed limit, how long will be take for the truck to stop if the maximum deceleration that can be achieved is -6 feet per second?
6. If the road contains a traffic light with the yellow light set for a duration of 5.5 seconds, at what speed should the truck be moving on the icy road to be traveling safely?
7. If the reaction time is assumed to be 0.5 seconds and $a = -16$ feet per second squared, find the minimum duration of a yellow light when the speed limit is 30 miles per hour and the intersection is 100 feet wide.
8. If the reaction time is assumed to be 0.75 seconds and $a = -22$ feet per second squared, find the minimum duration for a yellow light when the speed limit is 40 miles an hour and the intersection is 120 feet wide.

9. Derive a short formula for the minimum duration of a yellow light. Let w be the width of the intersection.

10. The yellow light at a midtown intersection with a 30-mph speed limit has a duration of 3 seconds. If a car traveling at 60 miles an hour is 300 feet from the intersection when the light turns yellow, can it safely stop or safely continue through the intersection? The intersection is 50 feet wide. Assume $a = -19.2$ ft./sec.^{2}

18

MAKING MONEY:
INVESTING IN A CERTIFICATE OF DEPOSIT

Description of the problem

You wish to buy a certificate of deposit. CDs are available with various rates of interest and with differing maturity periods. Which one should you choose if you want to invest $1000 for a period of five years?

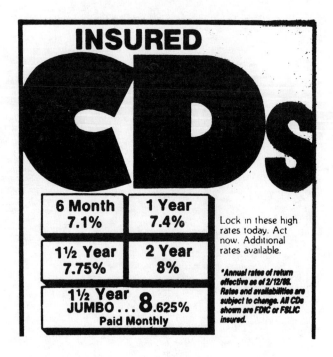

Mathematics concepts required:	Exponential functions
Appropriate for students in:	Algebra 2

Model

Suppose you are given $1000 to invest in a CD for five years. Two banks give the following information:

Bank A

Term	Annual Rate	Compounded	Effective Annual Yield
1. 6 months	6.95%	Quarterly	
2. 2 years	7.70%	Quarterly	
3. 4 years	8.10%	Quarterly	
4. 5 years	8.20%	Quarterly	

Bank B

Term	Annual Rate	Compounded	Effective Annual Yield
1. 6 months	6.90%	Daily	
2. 12 months	7.50%	Daily	
3. 18 months	7.70%	Daily	
4. 30 months	8.00%	Daily	
5. 60 months	8.15%	Daily	

Which CD would you choose?

To determine the best option for investing your money, Effective Annual Yield (EAY) should be used. EAY is the simple interest rate required to yield the same value at the end of one year as the advertised rate and compounding scheme will generate. Thus, EAY will allow for comparison of different rates and compounding schemes on the same scale. The formula for periodic compounding of interest is

$$V = P (1 + i/n)^{nt},$$

where V = value of CD, P = principal (i.e., amount invested), i = interest rate expressed as a decimal, n = frequency of compounding per year, and t = time in years.

Find the EAY for each of the examples above and round to the nearest hundredth of a percent.

Example: Bank A 1. One year, 6.95%, quarterly compounding

$$V = P \left(1 + \frac{0.0695}{4}\right)^{4(1)}$$

$$= P (1 + 0.017375)^4$$

$$= P (1.017375)^4$$

$$= P (1.071332416) \simeq P (1 + 0.0713) = P + 0.0713P$$

Effective Annual Yield $1.0713 - 1 = 0.0713$
Changing to a percent yields 7.13%

Finish the chart for the Effective Annual Yield. Any surprises?
Which CD would you choose?

You have $1000 to invest for five years. Try each CD to see how much
money you can make. Fill in the chart below, following the example.

Example: Bank A   1. Six months, 6.95%, quarterly

$$V = P \times \left(1 + \frac{0.0695}{4}\right)^{4 \times 5}$$

$$= 1000 \, (1.017375)^{20}$$

$$= 1000 \, (1.411306136)$$

$$= 1411.306136$$

$$= \$1411.31$$

CHART

Amount invested	Amount after 5 years	Amount of interest earned
Bank A		
1. $1000	$1411.31	$411.31
2.		
3.		
4.		
Bank B		
1.		
2.		
3.		
4.		
5.		

1. What is the smallest amount of interest earned?
2. What is the largest amount of interest earned?
3. Did the Effective Annual Yield help you in correctly comparing the
   various CDs?
4. Which CD would you choose? Why?
5. Is there any problem with this activity in comparing the CDs for five
   years?

For the daily compounding scheme, the EAY computation requires replacing *n* in the formula, with the number of days in a year, which is 365,
except during a leap year.

For example, if the interest rate is 8.15%, the formula becomes

$$V = P \left(1 + \frac{0.0815}{365}\right)^{365(1)} = P\,(1.0849)$$

$$= P + 0.0849\ P,\ \text{so the effective annual yield is 8.49\%.}$$

In order to increase the effective annual yield, some banks have adjusted the daily compounding formula by replacing the n inside the parentheses with 360, and the n in the exponent with 365. This formula is sometimes referred to as the *super interest* formula. With this scheme, the EAY calculation is

$$V = \left(1 + \frac{0.0815}{360}\right)^{365(1)} = P\,(1.0861)$$

$$= P + 0.0861\ P,\ \text{so the effective annual yield is 8.61\%.}$$

If daily compounding is available, you should ask which formula is used. The fine print on the CD will indicate that a 365/365 or a 365/360 formula is used.

Now compute the effective annual yield for each CD of bank B by using the super-interest formula.

19

POPULATION GROWTH IN THE UNITED STATES

Description of the problem

Knowing the size of a population is important to government planners for economic purposes, for national defense reasons, and for an adequate provision of public services, such as transportation facilities, schools, and hospitals. Historically, as populations grew, the relationships between population size and the consumption of natural resources was recognized. In the eighteenth century, Thomas R. Malthus, the British economist, published a book entitled *Essay on Population* (1798), in which he predicted that the world's population was growing at such an alarming rate that, within a century, it would outpace food production and cause massive starvation. Malthus's prediction of gloom and doom did not come true. Although Malthus's theories of population growth were not completely correct, he did point out that population growth could be modeled mathematically. Since his time, national planners and mathematicians have worked to devise models that could accurately predict the growth of various populations.

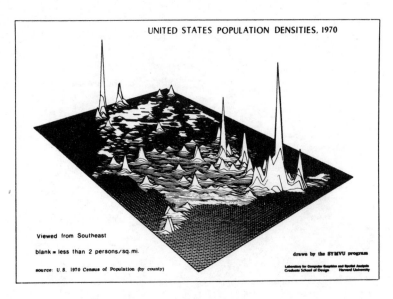

UNITED STATES POPULATION DENSITIES, 1970

Viewed from Southeast

blank = less than 2 persons/sq. mi.

source: U.S. 1970 Census of Population (by county)

drawn by the SYMVU program

Laboratory for Computer Graphics and Spatial Analysis
Graduate School of Design   Harvard University

Mathematics concepts required: Graphing, linear and parabolic equations

Appropriate for students in: Algebra 2

84

Model

The census results given below indicate the population of the United States from 1790 to 1950. Plot the results on a graph. Let the horizontal axis of the graph represent the years and the vertical axis represent the population in ten millions.

1950	150 697 000
1940	131 669 000
1930	122 775 000
1920	105 711 000
1910	91 972 000
1900	75 995 000
1890	62 948 000
1880	50 156 000
1870	38 558 000
1860	31 443 000
1850	23 192 000
1840	17 069 000
1830	12 866 000
1820	9 638 000
1810	7 240 000
1800	5 308 000
1790	3 929 000

1. Using your graph, attempt to obtain a linear model (linear equation) to predict the population size as a function of time. (*Hint*: Work with the portion of the graph that appears to be a straight line.) Use your model to predict the U.S. population in 1980. Find the actual value for the 1980 population and compute your error in terms of a percent of the actual population.

2. Use a quadratic model (parabola) to estimate the same population. Compute the resulting error. Is it greater or less than that obtained with the linear model? Explain the difference.

3. Malthus's theory of population growth states that a population's size increases according to a geometric progression. A mathematical model for geometric growth is supplied by the compound interest formula

$$A_t = p \, (1 + R)^t,$$

where A_t is the amount of money obtained after investing a principal of p at a rate in percent of R for a time of t. This model can be adopted for the study of population growth:

Let P_y = population size at year y
P_0 = population size at start of census taking

R = annual rate of population increase

t = number of years from first census to year y

Thus:

$$P_y = P_0 (1 + R)^t$$

Assume that the annual growth rate for the United States is 2 percent (0.02); use this model to find the population size in 1980. Compute the resulting error.

4. Use your plot of population growth to obtain estimates for the annual growth rate for the U.S. population. Obtain several estimates over different intervals. What is your conclusion about the annual growth rate of the U.S. population? Check the official growth rate in a U.S. almanac.

For further consideration

(Some knowledge of the exponential function is needed.) We have taken the U.S. census data from 1790 to 1950 and attempted to model the population growth of the United States using several simplistic approaches. Let us undertake the same task with a more sophisticated model, called the Verhulst(-Pearl) model:

$$P(t) = \frac{A}{B + (AP_0^{-1} - B)e_0^{-A(t - t_0)}},$$

where $P(t)$ = population size at year t, t_0 = reference year (1790), and A, B = parameters determined from data.

1. In 1850, Verhulst applied his model to U.S. 1790 to 1850 census data. From the data, he extrapolated the values of the parameters A and B, $A = 0.03134$ and $B = 1.5887 \times 10^{-10}$. Thus his model became

$$P(t) = \frac{313\ 400\ 000}{1.5887 + 78.7703e^{-0.03134(t - t_0)}}.$$

a. Check the accuracy of Verhulst's model by using it to compute at least three known values for the U.S. population. In each case, find the resulting error, if there is one. On the basis of your findings, does the model fit the data?

b. Use the model to estimate the U.S. population for 1980. Compute the resulting error, if there is one, and discuss possible reasons for it.

2. According to this model, when will the rate of growth of the U.S. population stop increasing or when did it stop increasing?

20

TRAJECTORY OF A CANNONBALL

Description of the problem

An ancient artillery piece has a muzzle velocity of 460 feet per second. Using various angles of barrel elevation, determine the range for cannonballs fired from this cannon if wind resistance is ignored.

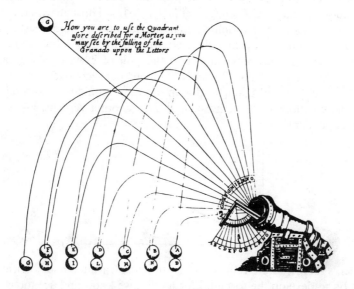

Mathematics concepts required: Radian measure, sine, cosine, velocity formulas

Appropriate for students in: Precalculus, trigonometry

Model

The introduction of the cannon as a weapon of warfare in the Middle Ages had a great impact on Western civilization. Besides altering the nature of warfare, the existence and use of cannons contributed to the decline of feudalism by breaching castle walls and reducing the protected isolation of the feudal lord from his people. As cannons became perfected, they could project a cannonball well beyond the view of the gunner. Methods were needed to assure accuracy in hitting distant, possibly unseen, targets. By using mathematics, natural scientists and mathematicians attempted to model the flight of a cannonball.

Niccolo Tartaglia (1500–1557), the Italian mathematician, realized that the range of a cannon shot was directly related to the angle of elevation of the cannon's barrel. Tartaglia devised a *gunner's quadrant*, an instrument that fits into the barrel of a gun and enables the gunner to determine the angle of barrel elevation and to calculate the approximate range. For a long time, the model used to determine range was based on the properties of a right triangle. The upward flight of the cannonball was the *hypotenuse*, the vertical leg was the distance it would drop onto the target, and the horizontal leg of the right triangle represented the range of the shot. The real scientific breakthrough in understanding the trajectories of cannonballs was made by the famous scientist, Galileo Galilei (1564–1642). Through experimentation and calculation, he determined that the idealized (wind-resistance neglected) trajectory of a projectile fired upward was a parabola, and that an upward-moving body was subject to the pull of gravity, which caused a downward acceleration of 32.2 feet per second per second (ft./sec.^{2}). Galileo demonstrated further that a motion in space, M, could be resolved into two separate components—one horizontal, H, the other vertical, V—and studied independently.

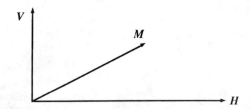

Galileo's theories were refined by his students, Cavalieri and Torricelli, who went on to develop the formulas for motion we know and use today.

Let us use Galileo's theories to study the firing behavior of an old cannon. Knowing the muzzle velocity, M (460 ft./sec.), and assigning an angle of barrel elevation, A, we can determine the horizontal distance (or range) that the projectile can be fired and the time to impact. We will devise a series of simple formulas whose numerical solutions can be easily found by using a calculator or computer.

Developing an algorithm

Step 1: Since we eventually wish to use a computer in our calculations, let us change the given angle of elevation A to radian R, as required by a computer:

$$R = A/57.2958$$

Step 2: To determine the upward velocity of a shot, we must take into account the vertical velocity of the projectile imparted by the gun and the effects of gravity on acceleration. Vertical velocity is a function of the muzzle velocity ($M = 460$) times the sin (R) minus the downward velocity due to gravity, $32.2T$. Thus:

$$V = M * SIN\ (R) - 32.2\ T$$

Step 3: Determine the time, TF, for the entire flight of a cannonball, by considering how the vertical velocity will behave during this flight. As the flight progresses, the vertical velocity will decrease until it reaches zero and the cannonball stops rising. Why? Then the cannonball will fall downward, increasing in velocity until it hits the ground. Thus:

$$TF = 2 * (M * SIN\ (R))/32.2$$

Step 4: To find the horizontal velocity of a shot, we rely on a function of muzzle velocity:

$$H = M * COS\ (R)$$

Step 5: Since the range, or total horizontal distance, traveled by the cannonball is equal to the total time times the horizontal velocity, we have the following:

$$D = H * TF$$

Step 6: In order to better understand the behavior of a cannonball's trajectory, complete the chart below, using the information we have just obtained.

CANNONBALL CHART

Angle (A)	Radian (R)	Total time (TF)	Horiz. velocity (H)	Range (D)
30	.523599	14.2857	398.3700	5691.00
32	.558505	15.1404	390.1022	5906.31
34	.593412	15.9764	381.3572	6092.71
36				
38				
40				
42				
44				
46				
48				
50				
52				
54				
56				
58				
60				

Develop a computer program to investigate further the relationship between the angle of elevation and the range. Allow the firing angle to vary in 2° increments between 10° and 75°, and print out the results in tabular form with an angle column and a range column.

Additional exercises

1. From the data you have generated, at what angle is the maximum range achieved?

2. Can the same range be obtained with different angles of barrel elevation? If so, is there a relationship between the angles?

3. Assume you are a gunner in the time of Tartaglia and obtain a table of barrel elevations and respective ranges for your cannon. You use the right-triangle model for the trajectory of a cannonball. Under what mathematical assumptions would this model be correct?

4. The *1989 Guiness Book of World Records* lists the longest javelin throw as 343 feet, 10 inches and the longest golf drive as 406 yards. Assuming that the athletes who accomplished these feats used the angle of projection necessary to obtain a maximum range, what respective velocities were imparted to the javelin and golf ball?

5. Devise and run a computer program that uses graphics to simulate the flight of a cannonball.

21

FOOD WEB OF SELECTED ANIMALS

Description of the problem

Because of damp, rainy weather, the insect population of an area has increased dramatically. The insects are annoying to people and animals. State authorities are in favor of using an insecticide that would literally wipe out the entire insect population. You, as an employee of the Environmental Protection Agency, must determine whether this action will be detrimental to the environment.

Mathematics concepts required: Simple matrix algebra

Appropriate for students in: Algebra 2

Model

The line diagram shown below is called a digraph and represents a small food web. The directed segment joining cat and rat, for example, indicates that cats eat rats. A number, 1, 2, or 3, is associated with each animal for later reference.

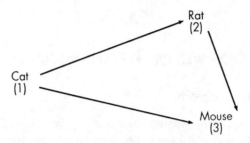

The relationships expressed in this digraph can be represented by a matrix if we let the numbers 1, 2, and 3 represent the respective rows and columns in a 3 × 3 matrix. In constructing a matrix to convey the information of the digraph, let the position for each entry be designated by the ordered pair (i, j), the i indicating the row position and the j indicating the column position, and where position (i, j) is filled in the following manner:

$$\text{position } (i, j) = \begin{cases} 1 \text{ if } i \text{ feeds on } j \\ 0 \text{ otherwise} \end{cases}$$

Thus, the matrix associated with the digraph above is $\begin{array}{c} 1 \\ 2 \\ 3 \end{array} \begin{bmatrix} 0 & 1 & 1 \\ 0 & 0 & 1 \\ 0 & 0 & 0 \end{bmatrix}$. Call

this matrix F. Notice that there are three 1's in the matrix representing the three directed segments of the digraph.

1. Find F^2 where $F^2 = F \cdot F$. The 1 in position $(1, 3)$ indicates that cats use mice as an indirect food source as well; that is, cats eat rats, and rats eat mice.

Consider the following digraph of a food web for seven animals, including the insects that are causing the problem.

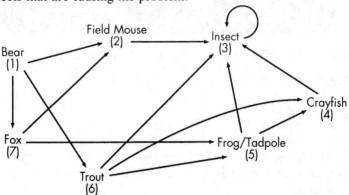

2. Construct the associated matrix to represent this web. Notice that rows 2 and 3 each contain a single 1, indicating that the associated animals have only a single food source. Column 1 contains all 0's. What does a column of all zeros indicate?

3. Notice that bears and trout have the most direct sources of food. This can be determined by finding the sums of the numbers in the rows. These sums indicate the number of direct food sources for each animal. Find the seven row sums.

4. Column 3 has the most 1's. What does this suggest about the food web?

The matrix F^2 denotes indirect (through one intermediary) sources of food.

5. Find F^2. Notice that column 3 contains all nonzero numbers. This indicates that all the animals rely on insects for food, either directly or indirectly.

6. Find $F + F^2$ and the associated row sums. This matrix denotes the total number of direct and indirect sources of food for each animal.

7. Which animal has the most food sources?

Let us now introduce the insecticide into the food web. Since the entire insect population will be killed, several animals will lose a source of food.

8. Construct a new matrix F' to represent the food web with no insects. Notice the effect this has on the overall animal population.

9. What has happened to the row sums? Since tadpoles and field mice rely solely on insects for their food, they, too, will soon die. This can be seen from their associated row sums.

10. Find F'^2 and $F' + F'^2$.

11. What are the row sums? Compare these answers with those of the original matrix F.

12. Will all the animals be affected by the insecticide? Which animal(s) will be least affected?

Organize and summarize your findings in a brief report to convince the authorities that this insecticide is harmful to the total environment.

22

WHICH CUP IS BEST?

Description of the problem

Hot coffee, placed in an insulated cup, cools over time to room temperature. Find the mathematical relationship between the temperature (T) of the coffee and the time (t) in minutes, where $t = 0$ when the coffee is poured into the cup. Will the functional relationship be essentially the same for ceramic, plastic, paper, and Styrofoam cups? Which cup is "best"?

Mathematics concepts required:	Functions—linear, power, exponential, logarithmic
Appropriate for students in:	Precalculus or calculus

Model

Background

Newton's law of cooling states that the rate of change of the temperature (T) of a heated object placed in a medium that has a constant temperature

T_M is proportional to the difference $T - T_M$. The resulting differential equation is

$$\frac{dT}{dt} = k(T - T_M),$$

where k depends on the heated material. The solution to the differential equation is

$$T = T_M + Ce^{kt}.$$

If T_0 represents the temperature of the object at $t = 0$, then $C = T_0 - T_M$, since $T_0 = T_M + Ce^{k \cdot 0} = T_M + C$. We know that k can be found if T is known for one other value of t. The resulting temperature curve will have the graph shown in figure 22.1. (Note that k is always negative.)

Fig. 22.1

If coffee is placed in a cup (with or without a lid), there is some insulation between the surrounding air and the hot coffee. Newton's law of cooling *may* not hold because of the insulation. The first project is to decide whether Newton's law holds. If it does not, the second project is to find the actual relationship between T and t, or a close approximation of it.

Procedure

A. Collect temperature data at 2-minute intervals for t between 0 and 20 minutes. The data points will have the form $(t, T - T_M)$.

B. Enter the data in column 3 below and compute the values in columns 2, 4, and 5.

t	$\ln t$	T	$T - T_M$	$\ln(T - T_M)$
0				
2				
4				
6				
8				
10				
12				
14				
16				
18				
20				

$$T_M = \text{_____(air temperature)}$$

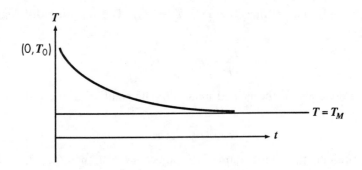

C. Plot the data points $(t, T - T_M)$ on
   1. regular graph paper,
   2. semilog paper, and
   3. log/log paper.
D. Select the plot that appears to be most linear. If—
   - (1) is the most linear graph, then the relationship is approximately
     $T = T_M + (at + b)$;
   - (2) is the most linear graph, then the relationship is approximately
     $T = T_M + b(a')$;
   - (3) is the most linear graph, then the relationship is approximately
     $T = T_M + bt^a$.

   The values for a and b will be found using linear regression, which is a procedure that selects a and b so that $y = ax + b$ fits the data points (x_1, y_1), $(x_2, y_2), \ldots, (x_n, y_n)$ best in the sense that $\sum_{i=1}^{n} [(ax_i + b) - y_i]^2$ is minimized.

By calculating the sum of the squares of the differences between the observed temperatures and the temperatures predicted for each of the equations 1, 2, and 3, the best relationship can be selected analytically to confirm the visual decision made from the graphs.

Suggestions for further study and potential extensions

Collect data and find the relationship between the speed of a bicycle and the stopping distance required if the back tire is skidded.

Appendix

1. WILDLIFE POPULATION SURVEY

Teacher's Guide

This model incorporates the use of a simple proportion into a nice sampling technique. Although some informal concepts of probability are used in this model, these concepts do not have to be stressed to the students. The teacher should prepare the fish pond and know how many fish are in the pond. The survey can use one or several shoe-box ponds with the class working as a whole or in small research groups. After the students finish their calculations and arrive at an estimate, the exact value of n can be given to them. This strategy provides a sense of anticipation in the students.

The sampling technique can be modified to include many situations that include other forms of wildlife, plants, and even people.

Answer to student assignment

To determine the numbers of different species of fish, follow the same sampling procedure. At the first tagging, note the numbers of each species tagged: blue gills, g; bass, b; and catfish, c. Apply the capture/recapture technique and at each time calculate three separate proportions, one for each species of fish.

REFERENCE

Knill, George. "Estimating the Size of Wildlife Populations." *Mathematics Teacher* 74 (October 1981): 548, 571.

2. PACK THEM IN

Teacher's Guide

Answers

Chart 1: Identical row alignment

Unit	Cost per Month	Number per Row	Rows	Layers	Total	Units Needed	Cost for Two Months
11 × 11	$ 67	5	5	3	75	3	$402
11 × 22	$105	11	5	3	165	2	$420
11 × 33	$130	16	5	3	240	1	$260

Chart 2: Staggered row alignment

Unit	Cost per Month	Number per Row	Rows	Layers	Total	Units Needed	Cost for Two Months
11 × 11	$ 67	5	6	3	90	2	$268
11 × 22	$105	11,10	3,3	3	189	1	$210
11 × 33	$130	16	6	3	288	1	$260

Answers to student assignment

1. From the information in your charts, what appears to be the least expensive way to store the containers?

   Answer: Staggered alignment in one 11 × 22 unit.

2. Would your decision be the same if the restriction of storing the containers in an upright position were removed?

   Answer: Yes. With either type of alignment (layer alignment now that cylinders are stored horizontally), it is possible to store 90 cylinders in an 11 × 11 unit, 18 cylinders in a layer stacked up to 5 high. Therefore, two 11 × 11 units are required for a total cost of $268, which is more than the cost of one 11 × 22 unit.

   For the 11 × 22 unit, with either type of layer alignment, a comparable floor plan will permit the storage of 200 cylinders. Consequently, the 11 × 22 unit is still best when horizontal storage is permitted, but either type of layer alignment can be used.

3. What is the second-best choice?

   Answer: One 11 × 33 unit.

3. COST OF A LONG-DISTANCE TELEPHONE CALL

Teacher's Guide

Background Presentation

1. Students should be familiar with the distance formula. Recall how it is derived.
2. Discuss uses of the distance formula:
   a) Mathematics formula
   b) Phone company
   c) Airlines

Presentation of the Model

The teacher presented this model in a lecture format using overhead transparencies rather than the worksheet package the students would actually use. Use this model as a reference and a guide.

1. To introduce the problem and provide motivation, use an overhead transparency of an actual phone bill that lists several long-distance phone calls to different places during the various rate periods.

2. Point out essential information on the bill referred to in the problem, such as the time, the place to which the call was made, the exchange number, the rate period (day, evening, or night/weekend), the number of minutes of the call, and the cost.

3. Show an overhead transparency of maps (figs. 3.1 and 3.2). Use the maps to explain how the Long Lines Department developed the V-H System that is used by phone companies today.

4. Use an overhead transparency of *V* and *H* coordinates (table 3.1), so that students can determine the distance between the two exchanges by applying the distance formula.

   a) Step 5 in the method accounts for the scale used by the Long Lines Department.

   b) The rounding suggested in the method is used by the phone company.

5. An overhead transparency of the student guide provides questions for this model.

6. Use an overhead transparency or use cost charts obtained from the phone company so that students can determine the cost of a call.

   Transparencies

   a) Phone bill

   b) Maps (figs. 3.1 and 3.2)

   c) *V* and *H* coordinates (table 3.1)

   d) Student guide

   e) Cost charts

Comments

The class was very interested in this model and the actual application of the distance formula.

REFERENCES

Bell Telephone Company of Pa. *Local and Joint Toll Tariffs, Pa.* PUS Toll No. 1A, 1D, 2C: 8 October 1986.

"The Telephone Rate Grid." *Mathematics Teacher* 73 (September 1980): 454–56.

Other sources of information

Bell of Pennsylvania
Strawberry Square
Harrisburg, PA 17101
(phone 1-800-548-4562)
Mr. V. R. Handwerk

A T & T
Consumer Market Sales Center
10802 Parkridge Boulevard
Reston, VA 22091

MCI Telecommunications Corporation
Mid Atlantic Division
230 Schilling Circle South
Hunt Valley, MD 21031

ITT United States Transmission Systems, Inc.
100 Plaza Drive
Secaucus, NJ 07096

4. THE GROCERY STORE PROBLEM

Teacher's Guide

Work with the students in a group setting to develop the 30-minute simulation shown. Have the students find a random-number table, or use a calculator with a random-number generator, to select 30 two-digit random numbers. Continue each simulation for 30 additional minutes. To select the better check-out system, ask the students to compare the average waiting times and the average line length for the 60-minute simulation. Are the results consistent with the 30-minute simulation?

REFERENCES

Biermann, Harold, Charles P. Bonini, and Warren H. Hausman. *Quantitative Analysis for Business Decisions.* Homewood, Ill.: Richard D. Irwin, 1977.

Sloyer, Clifford, Wayne Copes, William Sacco, and Robert Stark. *Queues.* Providence, R.I.: Janson Publications, 1987.

5. FACILITY LOCATION

Teacher's Guide

This is an excellent model for many levels of students. It was presented to a basic geometry class and discussed for one class period. The assignment was given as homework that night. A follow-up session to answer questions took about half a period the next day. When the model was presented, the students were asked to guess where the shelter should be located. A majority of them felt it should be located at the midpoint of the overall segment, so that point was included in all discussions in the model. After several guesses

were obtained, they were asked how to justify their answers, and together
we examined their suggestions for finding the total distance traveled. Eventually, the chart arrangement shown in the model developed naturally to
keep track of all our answers. Several students felt that locating the shelter
near the middle house was unfair because the student living there did not
have any distance to walk, while the students living on the end had a long
distance to walk. This led to a discussion of how changing the criteria
changes the answer.

Several important mathematical concepts can be emphasized in this
model. First, the concepts of distance on a number line, the midpoint of a
segment, and the relation of these simple geometric ideas to real problems
are emphasized. Second, the value of a chart that keeps track of a large
amount of information and analyzes it rapidly becomes self-evident. Third,
the value of graphs and the meaning of coordinates of a point can be
discussed in some detail when covering question 1 in the student assignment.

With classes that have a high ability level, it may be best to give the
problem to the students and allow them to work without any assistance for
a day or two before discussing it in class. Top-level classes could also be
asked to write a function that would determine the total distance traveled if
the shelter were located at any point on the road between the houses. This
could lead into discussions on the use of absolute value. An additional
challenge for these students is to consider the impact of one or more houses
having more than one student.

Answers to Questions in the Model

Completed Charts

Number of students	Shelter location	Total distance traveled
1. 3	A	$BA + CA = 500 + 600 = 1100'$
	M	$AM + BM + CM = 300 + 200 + 300 = 800'$
	B	$AB + CB = 500 + 100 = 600'$
	C	$AC + BC = 600 + 100 = 700'$
2. 5	A	$BA + CA + DA + EA = 2850'$
	M	$AM + BM + CM + DM + EM = 1425'$
	B	$AB + CB + DB + EB = 1350'$
	C	$AC + BC + DC + EC = 1250'$
	D	$AD + BD + CD + ED = 1450'$
	E	$AE + BE + CE + DE = 1900'$

3.	7	A	5400'
		B	2900'
		C	2600'
		M	2500'
		D	2400'
		E	2550'
		F	3450'
		G	3700'

In each case, the total distance traveled was at a minimum when the shelter was located at the middle house.

Answers to student assignment

1. Looking at the graphs of the other two situations, as shown below, we see that the lowest point on the graph is at the x-coordinate of the middle house. Thus, any other value picked for the location would be higher on the graph and would have a larger y-coordinate, or total-distance value.

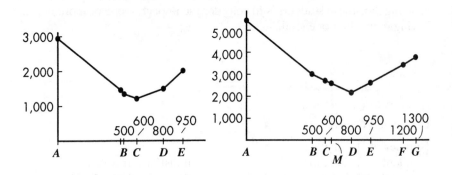

2. For an odd number of houses, the minimum total distance traveled will always occur when the shelter is located at the middle house.

3. Yes, the rule will still work. Total distances are as follows: at house A, 2050 ft.; at house B, 1800 ft.; at house C, 1650 ft.; at house D, 1600 ft.; at house E, 1650 ft.; at house F, 1800 ft.; and at house G, 7050 ft.

4. Setting up charts similar to the model, you will find the chart below. When looking at the chart, you will notice that the minimum distance traveled always occurs twice, at each of the two center houses. On further investigation, you should find that if you pick any point between the two center houses and calculate the total distance traveled,

Number of houses	Shelter location	Total distance
2	*A*	500'
	M (midpoint of *AB*)	500'
	B	500'
4	*A*	1900'
	M (midpoint of *AD*)	1300'
	B	900'
	C	900'
	D	1300'
6	*A*	4050'
	B	2050'
	C	1850'
	D	1850'
	E	2150'
	F	3150'

it will be the same as the distance at either center house. This is explained by looking at the graph as we did before. The graph for the situation with six houses is shown below. Notice that the segment joining the two center houses is a horizontal line and, hence, the *y*-coordinate, which represents the distance traveled, is the same anywhere on that segment. The minimum distance will occur if the shelter is built anywhere between the two center houses.

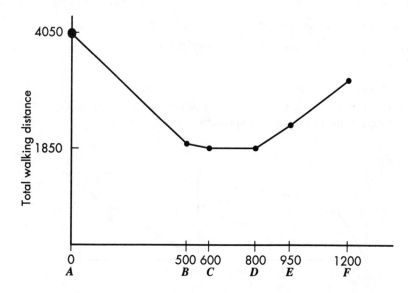

REFERENCE

Sloyer, Clifford. *Fantastiks of Mathematiks*. Providence, R.I.: Janson Publications, 1986.

6. TRAVELING WITH GRAPHS

Teacher's Guide

This exercise stresses the use of graphs as models and duplicates the historical investigations of velocity and acceleration. Natural philosophers and scientists, such as Nicole Oresme (1323–1382) and Galileo Galilei (1564–1642), used simple linear graphs to discover the properties of moving bodies. Students should be encouraged to make similar discoveries.

Answers to modeling exercise

1. Distance traveled during the first hour: $1/2 \times 1 \times 8 = 4$ miles
   Distance traveled during the last half hour: $1/2 \times 1/2 \times 8 = 2$ miles

2. Speed at the end of thirty minutes: 4 mph

3. Total distance: $4 + 16 + 2 = 22$ miles

4. Total distance: 29 miles

5. Three-and-a-half-hour trip: first hour
   Five-hour trip: first two hours and fourth hour

6. Three-and-a-half-hour trip: last half hour
   Five-hour trip: from second to third hour and fourth to fifth hour

7. Distance $= 1/2 \, vt$

Answers to student assignment

1. The slope of the line represents acceleration.

2. $a = v/t$

3. Distance $= 1/2 \, at^2$

4. Answers are open to discussion as to what a student thinks about the runner's performance. Two possible answers are these:

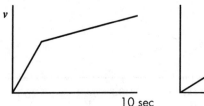
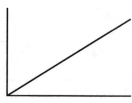

10 sec

5. Again, different answers are possible that would prompt classroom discussions. Possible answers are these:

25 minutes

a) Level ground

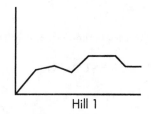

Hill 1

b) Cross-country

6. She accelerates at the beginning of the sled ride, then gradually slows up, and finally decelerates to a stop.

7. DELIVERING THE MAIL

Teacher's Guide

This problem is sufficiently straightforward for students to be able to develop the general solution with minimal guidance. After the problem is presented to the class, it will be valuable and necessary to spend time discussing assumptions on the nature of the street configuration. If the discussion does not lead to the simple configuration suggested in the first paragraph of the model description, introduce those assumptions.

It may be helpful to have the students solve the problem first for particular values of *W, n,* and *L.* Ask the students to research typical *W, n,* and *L* values in their community and then suggest two particular sets of realistic values for them to work with. Select one set of values so that $L/n > W$ and the other set so that $L/n < W$.

Solutions for the additional problems

1. If the mailboxes are not at the center of each lot but are located symmetrically across the street, the length of path A changes to $2L + W - 2d,$ where *d* is the distance from the last mailbox to the end of

the street. The length of path B does not change. The paths are equally short if

$$2L + W - 2d = nW + L.$$

The same type of analysis described in the model can be done using this *indifference* equation.

2. If the lot widths vary but the mailboxes are at the center of the front boundary of the lots, then the length of path A is again $2L + W - 2d$, where d has the same meaning as in (1) above. Path B has length $nW + L$. The analysis is therefore the same as for (1).

REFERENCE

Sloyer, Clifford. *Fantastiks of Mathematiks*. Providence, R.I.: Janson Publications, 1986.

8. THE GREENING OF FOREST ACRES

Teacher's Guide

Students could also be encouraged to graph their results to obtain a visual model of the customer/revenues relationship.

Answers to questions in the model

1. The number of customers that will supply the maximum revenues is 142.

2. Revenues for 141 customers equal $30 103.50
   Revenues for 142 customers equal $30 104.00
   Revenues for 143 customers equal $30 101.50

3. Yes, this proves the answer.

4. This is a discussion question prompting many answers; however, students should realize that the recruiting of customers must be stopped at some point or the contractor will lose money. The advertisement should include the phrase "for a limited time only" allowing the contractor to stop the discount process when he has a desired number of customers.

5. Revenues as a function of the number of customers is given by the following equations:

$$R = \$275C \text{ for } 1 \le C \le 100$$
$$R = \$(C)(425 - 1.50C) \text{ for } 100 < C \le 400$$

6. Allowing a discount of $1.75 for each enrollment over 120 customers, the revenue function becomes $R = (C)(485 - 1.75C)$ for $120 <$

$C \leq 400$, and the maximum revenue is $33 603.25, obtained with 139 customers.

9. JEEP IN THE DESERT

Teacher's Guide

The solution given is not the only solution yielding minimum fuel use. Before exposing students to the given solution, allow them to work in small groups for several class periods. A class discussion of strategy before they begin to work is advisable. Ask the students to try one or more of the following approaches:

A. Start with 500 gallons at the 0-mile marker and develop a strategy for transporting 50 gallons to the 500-mile marker. If a solution is found, ask the students to attempt to achieve the goal with fewer than 500 gallons.

B. Assume the supply points are equally spaced (for example, at 25-mile intervals) and develop a stockpiling strategy.

C. Give the students some hints that may lead to the solution presented above.

Students need to learn that *trial and revision* (a heuristic approach) is a legitimate mathematical procedure for developing a model to solve certain problems.

Suggestions for further study and potential extensions

After the students find a good solution or are shown the solution above, discuss whether the same procedures will yield a solution if the parameters of the problem—namely, miles per gallon, total distance, and fuel capacity—are changed.

REFERENCE

Cattel, Brad. "Letter to Editor." *Mathematics Teacher* 80 (April 1987): 270.

10. MANAGING A DEER POPULATION

Teacher's Guide

This computer simulation can become the basis for further study on the development and survival of wildlife populations. Classroom discussions should stress the need for wildlife management. The model can be adjusted to allow for such factors as a severe winter, during which 50 percent of the animal population dies, or illegal poaching, when 10 percent of the deer population is killed by poachers. By playing with this simulation and investigating several scenarios, students better appreciate the fragility of most wildlife resources. Using the principles established in this simulation, students can devise similar models for such resources as redwood forests, whale populations (statistics available from Greenpeace Foundation), or African elephant populations (statistics available from World Wildlife Federation).

Answers to student assignment

BASIC Program Solution

```
100 REM   SIMULATION PROGRAM FOR
110 REM   DEER POPULATION
120 REM   VERSION:       HARVESTING OF ZERO PERCENT
130 PRINT "ENTER NUMBER OF ADULT MALES:    ";
140 INPUT M
160 PRINT "ENTER NUMBER OF ADULT FEMALES: ";
170 INPUT F
180 PRINT
190 PRINT "ENTER NUMBER OF MALE FAWNS:       ";
200 INPUT C1
210 PRINT "ENTER NUMBER OF FEMALE FAWNS:   ";
220 INPUT C2
230 REM   MODEL ASSUMES TWO-THIRDS THE FAWNS
240 REM   ARE NEWBORN AND THE OTHERS ARE ONE YEAR OLD
250 REM
260 M1 = (2/3) * C1
270 M2 = C1 - M1
280 F1 = (2/3) * C2
290 F2 = C2 - F1
300 PRINT
305 PRINT
310 PRINT "          DEER POPULATION DISTRIBUTION"
320 PRINT "HERD", "ADULT", "ADULT", "MALE", "FEMALE"
330 PRINT "SIZE", "MALES", "FEMALES", "FAWNS ", "FAWNS "
340 FOR I = 1 TO 65
350    PRINT "-";
360 NEXT I
370 PRINT
380 FOR Y = 1 TO 11
390    S = M + F + M1 + F1 + M2 + F2
400    PRINT INT(S), INT(M), INT(F), INT(M1 + M2), INT(F1 + F2)
410    T1 = M
420    T2 = F
430    T3 = M1
440    T4 = F1
450    T5 = M2
460    T6 = F2
470    M  = .9 * T1 + .6 * T5
480    F  = .9 * T2 + .6 * T6
490    M1 = .48 * T2
500    F1 = .42 * T2
510    M2 = .5 * T3
520    F2 = .5 * T4
530 NEXT Y
540 END
```

Deer Population Distribution

```
ENTER NUMBER OF ADULT MALES:        ?      1703
ENTER NUMBER OF ADULT FEMALES:      ?      3714

ENTER NUMBER OF MALE FAWNS:         ?      2058
ENTER NUMBER OF FEMALE FAWNS:       ?      1920
```

DEER POPULATION DISTRIBUTION

HERD SIZE	ADULT MALES	ADULT FEMALES	MALE FAWNS	FEMALE FAWNS
9395	1703	3714	2058	1920
10339	1944	3726	2468	2199
10924	2161	3737	2680	2345
11353	2480	3832	2688	2352
11818	2768	3918	2736	2394
12278	3030	3997	2800	2450
12720	3278	4080	2859	2501
13153	3515	4166	2918	2553
13578	3739	4253	2979	2606
13998	3953	4342	3041	2661
14412	4157	4432	3105	2716

Ok

1. To allow for an annual hunting harvest of 78 percent of male deer, program line 470 should be modified to read:

$$M = .9 * T1 + .6 * T5 - .78 * T1$$

BASIC Program Solution with 78 Percent Male Harvest

```
540 END
100 REM   SIMULATION PROGRAM FOR
110 REM   DEER POPULATION
120 REM   VERSION:   HARVESTING OF 78% OF MALES
130 PRINT "ENTER NUMBER OF ADULT MALES:      ";
140 INPUT M
160 PRINT "ENTER NUMBER OF ADULT FEMALES: ";
170 INPUT F
180 PRINT
190 PRINT "ENTER NUMBER OF MALE FAWNS:     ";
200 INPUT C1
210 PRINT "ENTER NUMBER OF FEMALE FAWNS:     ";
220 INPUT C2
230 REM   MODEL ASSUMES TWO-THIRDS THE FAWNS
240 REM   ARE NEWBORN AND THE OTHERS ARE ONE YEAR OLD
250 REM
260 M1 = (2/3) * C1
270 M2 = C1 - M1
280 F1 = (2/3) * C2
290 F2 = C2 - F1
300 PRINT
305 PRINT
```

```
310 PRINT "          DEER POPULATION DISTRIBUTION"
320 PRINT "HERD", "ADULT", "ADULT", "MALE", "FEMALE"
330 PRINT "SIZE", "MALES", "FEMALES", "FAWNS ", "FAWNS "
340 FOR I = 1 TO 65
350     PRINT "-";
360 NEXT I
370 PRINT
380 FOR Y = 1 TO 11
390     S = M + F + M1 + F1 + M2 + F2
400     PRINT INT(S), INT(M), INT(F), INT(M1+M2), INT(F1+F2)
410     T1 = M
420     T2 = F
430     T3 = M1
440     T4 = F1
450     T5 = M2
460     T6 = F2
470     M  = .9 * T1 + .6 * T5 - .78 * T1
480     F  = .9 * T2 + .6 * T6
490     M1 = .48 * T2
500     F1 = .42 * T2
510     M2 = .5 * T3
520     F2 = .5 * T4
530 NEXT Y
540 END
```

Deer Population Distribution

ENTER NUMBER OF ADULT MALES:	?	1703
ENTER NUMBER OF ADULT FEMALES:	?	3714
ENTER NUMBER OF MALE FAWNS:	?	2058
ENTER NUMBER OF FEMALE FAWNS:	?	1920

DEER POPULATION DISTRIBUTION

HERD SIZE	ADULT MALES	ADULT FEMALES	MALE FAWNS	FEMALE FAWNS
9395	1703	3714	2058	1920
9011	615	3726	2468	2199
9248	485	3737	2680	2345
9466	593	3832	2688	2352
9657	607	3918	2736	2394
9859	611	3997	2800	2450
10066	625	4080	2859	2501
10277	639	4166	2918	2553
10491	652	4253	2979	2606
10711	665	4342	3041	2661
10934	679	4432	3105	2716

Ok

2. To allow for an annual hunting harvest of 50 percent male deer and 50 percent female deer, program lines 470 and 480 should be modified to read:

$$470 \ M = .9 * T1 + .6 * T5 - .5 * T1$$
$$480 \ F = .9 * T2 + .6 * T6 - .5 * T2$$

BASIC Program Solution with 50 Percent Male and Female Harvest

```
100 REM SIMULATION PROGRAM FOR
110 REM DEER POPULATION
120 REM VERSION:    HARVESTING OF 50% OF MALES AND 50% OF FEMALES
130 PRINT "ENTER NUMBER OF ADULT MALES:      ";
140 INPUT M
160 PRINT "ENTER NUMBER OF ADULT FEMALES: ";
170 INPUT F
180 PRINT
190 PRINT "ENTER NUMBER OF MALE FAWNS:        ";
200 INPUT C1
210 PRINT "ENTER NUMBER OF FEMALE FAWNS:    ";
220 INPUT C2
230 REM MODEL ASSUMES TWO-THIRDS THE FAWNS
240 REM ARE NEWBORN AND THE OTHERS ARE ONE YEAR OLD
250 REM
260 M1 = (2/3) * C1
270 M2 = C1 - M1
280 F1 = (2/3) * C2
290 F2 = C2 - F1
300 PRINT
305 PRINT
310 PRINT "        DEER POPULATION DISTRIBUTION"
320 PRINT "HERD", "ADULT", "ADULT", "MALE", "FEMALE"
330 PRINT "SIZE", "MALES", "FEMALES", "FAWNS ", "FAWNS "
340 FOR I = 1 TO 65
350     PRINT "-";
360 NEXT I
370 PRINT
380 FOR Y = 1 TO 11
390     S = M + F + M1 + F1 + M2 + F2
400     PRINT INT(S), INT(M), INT(F), INT(M1 + M2), INT(F1 + F2)
410     T1 = M
420     T2 = F
430     T3 = M1
440     T4 = F1
450     T5 = M2
460     T6 = F2
470     M = .9 * T1 + .6 * T5 - .5 * T1
480     F = .9 * T2 + .6 * T6 - .5 * T2
490     M1 = .48 * T2
500     F1 = .42 * T2
510     M2 = .5 * T3
520     F2 = .5 * T4
530 NEXT Y
540 END
```

Deer Population Distribution

ENTER NUMBER OF ADULT MALES:	?	1703
ENTER NUMBER OF ADULT FEMALES:	?	3714
ENTER NUMBER OF MALE FAWNS:	?	2058
ENTER NUMBER OF FEMALE FAWNS:	?	1920

DEER POPULATION DISTRIBUTION

HERD SIZE	ADULT MALES	ADULT FEMALES	MALE FAWNS	FEMALE FAWNS
9395	1703	3714	2058	1920
7631	1092	1869	2468	2199
5334	848	1131	1788	1565
3654	874	920	991	867
2560	618	603	713	624
1752	410	384	510	446
1183	296	269	329	288
805	205	183	221	193
546	137	121	153	133
369	93	82	102	89
249	64	56	69	60

Ok

11. GETTING THE WORD OUT

Teacher's Guide

This problem is solved by a process called *linear programming*. The fact that the solution occurs at a corner point follows from the desire to have the objective function, with its given slope, pass through the feasibility region and have the greatest possible *y*-intercept. It is also true that the objective function takes on its minimum value over the region at a corner point.

Linear programming is a recent addition to the high school curriculum, and many algebra texts include it.

Possible extensions of this model include the following:

1. Add more conditions to the model to create a feasibility region with more (or fewer) corner points. For example, suppose the total number of ads cannot exceed 70.

2. Contact local radio and television stations and inquire about determining factors for the cost of advertising.

3. Assume that the promoter also wishes to use newspaper ads at $125 each and she wishes to use no more than 5 such ads. Modify the model to allow for newspaper advertising and solve under the original constraints.

Answers to student assignment

1. 1710 seconds

2. $19 600

3. 53 radio ads and 15 TV ads

REFERENCES

Dolciani, Mary, John Graham, Richard Swanson, and Sidney Sharron. *Algebra 2 and Trigonometry*. Boston: Houghton-Mifflin Co., 1986.

Mizrahi, Abe, and Michael Sullivan. *Finite Mathematics with Applications for Business and Social Sciences*. 2d ed. New York: John Wiley & Sons, 1976.

12. AN IRRIGATION PROBLEM

Teacher's Guide

Suggestions for introducing the model

Spend up to one period discussing the problem. Involve students in the process of checking the graph of $C(x)$. Make sure they understand how the objective of uniform coverage translates into mathematical terms.

Give the students several days to work in teams to complete the table. If any students are capable, encourage the production of a computer code to do the calculations.

Spend one period in class with students working in teams to find the speed of the device across the field.

Answers to questions in the model

1. Optimal $d = 35'$.
2. Twenty-nine sprinklers are needed.
3. Place the unit ten feet from the field edge.
4. The speed of the device across the field is 12.85 feet per hour.
5. The maximum amount of water is 1.19 inches.
6. The minimum amount of water is 0.81 inches.

Answer to suggestion for further study

If triple overlap is permitted, more uniform coverage can be obtained.

1. Optimal $d = 17.5'$.
2. Fifty-seven sprinklers are needed.
3. Place the unit ten feet from the field edge.
4. The speed of the device across the field is 28.4 feet per hour.
5. The maximum amount of water is 1.10 inches.
6. The minimum amount of water is 0.90 inches.

13. PAPER ROLLS

Teacher's Guide

To motivate the students, show them a roll of cash-register paper and ask them to think of ways to find the number of feet of paper on the roll. Discuss the impact on the answer if the paper thickness is not measured accurately. Use a good quality micrometer to estimate the paper thickness by measuring a stack 10- or 20-wraps thick.

The cable-wrapping problem can be solved with a calculator. However, this problem is an excellent computer-programming project and an opportunity for the mathematics and computer-science teachers and classes to interact.

14. WHEN FOUR EQUALS THREE EQUALS TWO

Teacher's Guide

The completed table for Tim's Toy Company is as follows:

Group orderings

MAN ADV SAL TIM	ADV MAN SAL TIM	SAL MAN ADV TIM	TIM MAN ADV SAL
MAN ADV TIM SAL	ADV MAN TIM SAL	SAL MAN TIM ADV	TIM MAN SAL ADV
MAN SAL ADV TIM	ADV SAL MAN TIM	SAL ADV MAN TIM	TIM ADV MAN SAL
MAN SAL TIM ADV	ADV SAL TIM MAN	SAL ADV TIM MAN	TIM ADV SAL MAN
MAN TIM ADV SAL	ADV TIM MAN SAL	SAL TIM MAN ADV	TIM SAL MAN ADV
MAN TIM SAL ADV	ADV TIM SAL MAN	SAL TIM ADV MAN	TIM SAL ADV MAN

Solutions to the problems

1. (a) [5; 4,4,1] $I = (1/3, 1/3, 1/3)$
   (b) [25; 24,21,4] $I = (1/3, 1/3, 1/3)$

2. *Jim's Junk Company*

Coll(3)	Dist(3)	Jim(1)	Total	Result
Yes	Yes	Yes	7	Pass
Yes	Yes	No	6	Pass
Yes	No	Yes	4	Pass
No	Yes	Yes	4	Pass
Yes	No	No	3	Fail
No	Yes	No	3	Fail
No	No	Yes	1	Fail
No	No	No	0	Fail

$$I_{Jim} = (1/3, 1/3, 1/3)$$

Tim's Toy Company

Man(2)	Adv(2)	Sal(2)	Tim(1)	Total	Result
Yes	Yes	Yes	Yes	7	Pass
Yes	Yes	Yes	No	6	Pass
Yes	Yes	No	Yes	5	Pass
Yes	No	Yes	Yes	5	Pass
No	Yes	Yes	Yes	5	Pass
Yes	Yes	No	No	4	Pass
Yes	No	Yes	No	4	Pass
Yes	No	No	Yes	3	Fail
No	Yes	Yes	No	4	Pass
No	Yes	No	Yes	3	Fail
No	No	Yes	Yes	3	Fail
Yes	No	No	No	2	Fail
No	Yes	No	No	2	Fail
No	No	Yes	No	2	Fail
No	No	No	Yes	1	Fail
No	No	No	No	0	Fail

$$I_{\text{Tim}} = (1/3, 1/3, 1/3, 0)$$

The Banzhaf and Shapley-Shubik Indexes are the same for each of the companies. In general, however, they are not necessarily the same. Consider the game [6; 5,4,1].

REFERENCES

Lucas, William F. "Measuring Power in Weighted Voting Systems." In *Case Studies in Applied Mathematics*. Washington, D.C.: Mathematical Association of America, 1976.

Shapley, L. S. "A Value for *n*-Person Games." In *Contributions to the Theory of Games, II*, Annals of Mathematical Studies, No. 28, edited by N. W. Kuhn and A. W. Tucker, pp. 307–17. Princeton, N.J.: Princeton University Press, 1953.

Shapley, L. S., and Martin Shubik. "A Method for Evaluating the Distribution of Power in a Committee System." *American Political Science Review* 48 (1954): 787–92.

15. TIME TO WASTE

Teacher's Guide

1. The York County Planning Commission's estimates for the amount of garbage produced in a day are as follows:

    1995—831 tons a day
    2000—807 tons a day

Ask the students to compare their predictions with those of the planning commission. Discuss the possible reasons for the discrepancies.

2. Ask the students to collect data on garbage production in their area and to make predictions on future production rates. If possible, involve the science department in a discussion on the merits of various alternatives for handling garbage.

Answers to student assignment

All answers are approximate, based on computer-program estimates.

1. 771 tons a day
2. 870 (1027 with bottles and cans)
3. 826
4. 22 percent
5. Approximately 5.6 to 5.9 pounds per person per day
6. York County produced 4.65 pounds per person per day, which is much higher than the U.S. average.

16. STREET PARKING

Teacher's Guide

This model should be used after students are able to work with trigonometric functions with relative ease. The model has been designed for the students to work through the project alone. An oral description of the problem could be given before the sheets are distributed to the class.

To give more choices in the final parking design, the width of the street may be made wider or narrower than the 60 feet given in the problem. With some choices, only one type of parking can be accommodated.

As an extension of this problem, students can examine the efficiency of their school parking lot. Is it well designed? If not, how could it be improved? A local mall parking lot can also be examined. In this large situation, what allowances are made for traffic flow, handicapped parking, and so on? Research projects on parking-lot design can be assigned for small-group investigation.

Solutions and answers to the questions in the model

1. 33
2. $60 - 20 = 40$; yes
3. $c = 10/\sin \phi$

4.

ϕ	c	Cars/side
10	57.6	9
15	38.6	13
20	29.2	18
25	23.7	22
30	20	26
45	14.1	37
60	11.5	45
75	10.4	50
90	10	52

5. 90°. It is difficult to enter a space that is perpendicular to the traffic flow.

6. $x = 10/\tan \phi$

7. $x + 16$

8. $d = (x + 16) \sin \phi$

9.

ϕ	x	d
10	56.7	12.6
15	37.3	13.8
20	27.5	14.9
25	21.4	15.8
30	17.3	16.7
45	10	18.4
60	5.8	18.9
75	2.7	18.1
90	—	16

10.

ϕ	$60 - 2d$
10	34.8
15	32.4
20	30.2
25	28.4
30	26.6
45	23.2
60	22.2
75	23.8
90	28

11. Answers will vary.

17. YELLOW TRAFFIC LIGHTS

Teacher's Guide

A graph of the yellow-light duration as a function of the initial velocity is interesting. If the students are each given a different velocity, the calculations will not be too burdensome. Using this graph, students can answer questions about the effects of traveling above or below the speed limit when the light turns yellow. For example: If one is traveling ten miles below the speed limit, under what conditions is it possible to clear the intersection before the light turns red?

The following derivations of equations (1) and (2) may be useful for some students. The equations can be derived from these basic formulas:

$$v_m = x/t \tag{i}$$
$$a = (v - v_0)/t \tag{ii}$$
$$v_m = \frac{v + v_0}{2}, \tag{iii}$$

where v_m represents the average velocity over time t, v_0 represents the velocity at the beginning of time t, and v represents the velocity at time t.

Equation (1): $x = v_0 t + 1/2\ at^2$ may be derived by using a geometric speed-time model (see module) or in the following manner:

$$x = v_m t \text{ from (i)}$$
$$= \left(\frac{v + v_0}{2}\right) t \text{ from (iii)}$$
$$= \left(\frac{v_0 + at + v_0}{2}\right) t, \text{ since } v = v_0 + at \text{ from (ii)}$$

Therefore, $x = v_0 t + 1/2\ at^2$.

Equation (2): $v^2 = v_0^2 + 2ax$ can be obtained as follows:

$$x = \left(\frac{v + v_0}{2}\right) t$$
$$ax = \left[\frac{(v - v_0)}{t}\right]\left[\frac{v + v_0}{2}\right] t$$
$$\text{and } 2ax = v^2 - v_0^2$$

Solutions to student assignment

1. Since 1 mile = 5280 feet, then 45 miles = 237 600 feet; 60 seconds = 1 minute, then 3600 seconds = 1 hour. Thus 237 600 ÷ 3600 = 66 feet a second.

2. Results determined individually

3. No, he will need approximately 380 feet to stop.

4. *a*) 17.93 feet   *b*) 161 feet

5. 6.11 seconds

6. Approximately 40 miles an hour

7. 4.14 seconds

8. 4.13 seconds

9. $\dfrac{-v/(-2a) + v\,(t) + w}{v}$

10. No

REFERENCES

Shonle, John. *Environmental Applications of Physics.* Reading, Mass.: Addison-Wesley Publishing Co., 1975.

Smith, Alpheus, and John Cooper. *Elements of Physics.* New York: McGraw-Hill, 1977.

18. MAKING MONEY: INVESTING IN A CD

Teacher's Guide

The background needed for this model is a simple- and compound-interest unit, as would normally appear in a business math class. The compound-interest formula furnishes a good opportunity for students to work with exponential expressions and to practice using a scientific calculator.

Ask the students to find bank or savings-and-loan advertisements in local newspapers and to check the accuracy of the effective annual yields listed. Challenge the students to find an institution that offers "super interest." Ask one or two banks to give you a copy of the fine print on a CD that offers daily compounding.

Thoroughly discuss the value of EAY in comparing CDs. For the best students in the class, a project could be to find several examples where comparing interest rates instead of EAYs will lead to a decision that will not produce the most interest.

Answers to questions in the model

Effective Annual Yield

Bank A	Bank B
1. 7.13%	1. 7.14%
2. 7.93%	2. 7.79%
3. 8.35%	3. 8.00%
4. 8.46%	4. 8.34%
	5. 8.49%

Chart (last 2 columns)

Amount after 5 years	Interest earned
Bank A	
1. $1411.31	$411.31
2. $1464.25	$464.25
3. $1493.25	$493.25
4. $1500.58	$500.58
Bank B	
1. $1411.94	$411.94
2. $1454.94	$454.94
3. $1469.55	$469.55
4. $1491.76	$491.76
5. $1502.99	$502.99

1. Smallest—$411.31

2. Largest—$502.99

3. Yes

4. Bank B, #5

5. A certificate whose term is less than five years will need to be renewed one or more times and the interest rate may change. The only rates guaranteed for five years are on CDs with five-year terms.

REFERENCE

Hartzler, J. S. "When Is One Not Equal to One?" *Mathematics Teacher* 77 (April 1984): 274–76.

19. POPULATION GROWTH IN THE UNITED STATES

Teacher's Guide

In this module, the sequencing of exercises is important. It illustrates a natural modeling procedure. Instructional sequencing moves from the plotting of data and the construction of a visual model (graph) to the use of visual or mathematical linear curve fitting to arrive at a linear model (equation) for the estimation of U.S. population growth. How appropriate is this model? Does it serve for approximation purposes? The plot of the actual data yields a curved line for a graph. How might the curved line be approximated? (Parabola)

Malthus's original premise was that the population growth was geometric. The curve supplied by the data is really an exponential curve. Exponential growth can be explored using the compound-interest formula as indicated. However, this model is also simplistic in its assumption of growth rate being constant. The population growth rate is not constant, and population growth is not unbounded. Population behavior is dependent on many factors, both social and political. Students should discuss some of these factors in their examination of population growth. Consideration of the Verhulst-Pearl model supplies a realistic behavior pattern for U.S. population growth through the 1960s, but it appears to have lost its accuracy for more recent population estimates. Modeling population growth is a complex and difficult task and is still in the process of being resolved.

This series of exercises duplicates the historical modeling process for population growth, that is, the use of linear equations → higher-order polynomial equations → exponential equations → logistic equations.

Answers to questions in the model

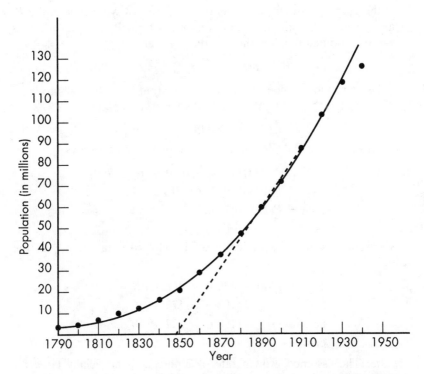

1. Using the graph shown above, a linear approximation is established over the range of $1845 \le t \le 1950$. Using the slope-point form of the equation for a straight line, we get

$$m = \frac{\Delta P}{\Delta t} = \frac{76 - 50}{1900 - 1880} = \frac{26}{20} = 1.3.$$

Using the point (1930, 123), we get

$$1.3 = \frac{P - 123}{t - 1930}$$

or

$$1.3 \, (t - 1930) = P - 123.$$

Thus $P = 1.3t - 2386$. Written as a function of t, this becomes

$$P(t) = 1.3t - 2386$$
$$\text{and } P(1980) = 188 \times 10^6;$$
$$\text{actual—} \quad P(1980) = 227 \times 10^6;$$
$$\text{error—} \qquad\quad 17\%.$$

2. If the graph is visualized as an arc of a parabola symmetric to the P-axis, then the parabolic equation is of the form $P = P_0 + at^2$. This can be modified to allow the t reading in years:

$$P = P_0 + a(t - t_0)^2 \text{ or } P_0 + a(t - 1790)^2$$

Use a rounded value of the 1790 population (i.e., 4×10^6) to let $P_0 = 4$, and then using the point (1890, 63), we obtain

$$63 = 4 + a \, (1890 - 1790)^2,$$

from which $a = 0.0059$. Thus, P as a function of t becomes

$$P(t) = 4 + 0.0059 \, (t - 1790)^2$$
$$P(1980) = 217 \times 10^6$$
$$\text{actual—} \quad P(1980) = 227 \times 10^6$$
$$\text{error—} \qquad\quad 4\%.$$

A parabola provides a better fit to the plotted data curve than the straight line.

3.
$$P(1980 - 1790) = 4(1.02)^{190}$$
$$P(1980) = 172 \times 10^6$$
$$\text{actual—} \quad P(1980) = 227 \times 10^6$$
$$\text{error—} \qquad 24\%$$

Note: The assumed growth rate of 2 percent is artificially large for illustrative purposes.

4. The growth rate is not constant.

Solutions for further consideration

1. *a*) $P(1950) = 148 \times 10^6$ 1% error
   $P(1900) = 77 \times 10^6$ 1% error

$$P(1850) = 23 \times 10^6 \quad \text{less than 1\% error}$$

$$b)\ P(1980) = \frac{313\ 400\ 000}{1.5887 + 78.7703e^{-0.03134(190)}}$$

$$P(1980) = 175 \times 10^6 \quad 23\% \text{ error}$$

Although the model supplies accurate population estimates up through 1950, in more recent years it appears to underestimate the size of the U.S. population. Perhaps social and economic factors in post–World War II America have resulted in a population boom—one that could not be predicted even with a mathematical model.

2. Using the model, we see that populations can be estimated for various years and the results can be plotted on a graph. The inflection point of the graph will indicate when the population growth rate stopped increasing. Exact calculations have indicated that this happened 1 April 1914.

The equation for the Verhulst model, if graphically plotted, gives rise to an S-shaped curve known as a *logistic curve* (which is from the Greek *logistikos*, meaning rational). Other modeling situations also follow a logistic curve; for example, the dissemination of technological innovations and the spread of a disease. These situations can be modeled and studied by using Verhulst-like equations.

REFERENCES

Spiegel, Murray R. *Applied Differential Equations*. Englewood Cliffs, N.J.: Prentice-Hall, 1981.

Tierney, John A. *Differential Equations*. Newton, Mass.: Allyn & Bacon, 1979.

Woodward, Ernest, and Thomas Hamel. "Calculator Lessons Involving Population, Inflation, and Energy." *Mathematics Teacher* 72 (September 1979): 450–57.

20. TRAJECTORY OF A CANNONBALL

Teacher's Guide

This exercise furnishes historical insights into the concept of mathematical modeling. The fact that mathematical models were used in the Middle Ages is revealing—mathematical modeling is not something new! "How accurate is the right-triangle model for a trajectory? What does accuracy mean in sixteenth-century artillery terms?" are some questions that evolve from this exercise. Galileo's work on trajectories introduced the mathematical concept of vectors, and the aiming of early artillery led to developments in trigonometry.

In step 3, we determine TF by realizing that when the cannonball reaches its maximum height, it stops, that is, $V = 0$ or $M * \sin(R) - 32.2\ T = 0$, and solving for T, we find $T = \dfrac{M * \sin{(R)}}{32.2}$. Since the cannonball falls to the ground in the same time, the time for the whole flight TF is

$$2 \times \dfrac{M * \sin{(R)}}{32.2}.$$

BASIC Program for Artillery Range

```
100 HOME
110 GOSUB 120
120 PRINT : PRINT : PRINT
130 GOSUB 250
140 HOME
150 GOSUB 360
160 GOSUB 480
170 END
180 PRINT "ARTILLERY RANGE"
190 PRINT
200 PRINT "DISTANCE TO THE POINT OF IMPACT"
210 PRINT "FOR AN ARTILLERY SHELL HAVING"
220 PRINT "GIVEN MUZZLE VELOCITY AND ANGLES"
230 PRINT "OF ELEVATION"
240 RETURN
250 PRINT
260 INPUT "MUZZLE VELOCITY (FEET/SEC)" :M
270 PRINT
280 PRINT "ANGLES IN DEGREES"
290 PRINT
300 INPUT "LOWER LIMIT ":A1
310 PRINT
320 INPUT "UPPER LIMIT ":A2
330 PRINT
340 INPUT "INCREMENT SIZE OF ANGLE ":A3
350 RETURN
360 PRINT
370 PRINT "ANGLE", "DISTANCE (FEET)"
380 FOR A = A1 TO A2 STEP A3
390 R = A / 57.2958
400 H = M * COS (R)
410 TF = 2 * (M * SIN (R))/32.2
420 D = H * TF
430 D = INT (100 * D + .5) / 100
440     PRINT A,D
450     NEXT A
460     RETURN
470     PRINT
480     INPUT "TRY ANOTHER SET OF DATA (Y/N)" ;U$
490     IF U$ = "Y" THEN 100
500     IF U$ = "N" THEN 170
510     PRINT "INVALID RESPONSE" : GOTO 480
```

Answers to additional exercises

1. A 45° angle results in maximum range. Tartaglia was the first person to discover this fact.

2. Yes. The same range can be achieved by using angles that are comple-
ments of each other, that is, 60° and 30°, 20° and 70°, and so on.

3. If one fires a projectile with velocity M at barrel angle θ and employs
a right-triangle model, assuming the range is correctly known to be
$(M \cos \theta)T$, then the following mathematical situation results:

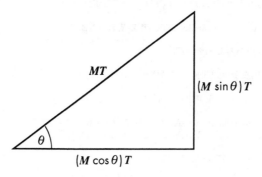

Thus,
$$(MT)^2 = [(M \cos \theta)T]^2 + [(M \sin^2 \theta)T]^2$$
$$(MT)^2 = (MT)^2 (\cos^2\theta + \sin^2\theta)$$
$$(MT)^2 = (MT)^2.$$

Two erroneous assumptions are made:

1. Acceleration of gravity is neglected.

2. The time for the cannonball to go up and down is $2T$, whereas
the time for the horizontal distance is T—the times should be the
same.

4. Javelin:
$$TF = 2 * (M * \sin 45°)/32.2$$
$$= 2 * (M * 0.7071)/32.2$$
$$TF = 0.0439M$$
$$H = M * \cos 45° = M * 0.7071$$
$$H = 0.7071M$$
$$D = H * TF = 343.833 \text{ ft.}$$
$$(0.0439\ M)(0.7071\ M) = 343.833 \text{ ft.}$$
$$0.031\ M^2 = 343.833 \text{ ft.}$$
$$M = 105.32 \text{ ft./sec.}$$

Golf ball: $D = H * TF = 1218 \text{ ft.}$
$$0.031\ M^2 = 1218 \text{ ft.}$$
$$M = 198.22 \text{ ft./sec.}$$

5. Programs may vary to allow for creativity. One possible program follows:

Program for the Trajectory of a Cannonball

```
100  REM CANNON
110  HOME
112  PRINT : PRINT
120  PRINT "THIS PROGRAM MODELS THE IDEAL"
123  PRINT
125  PRINT "FLIGHT OF A PROJECTILE AS FIRED"
128  PRINT
130  PRINT "FROM A CANNON IN THE X-Y PLANE"
135  PRINT
140  PRINT "YOU WILL SPECIFY:"
145  PRINT
150  PRINT "(1) LOCATION OF CANNON IN X-Y PLANE"
155  PRINT
160  PRINT "(2) INITIAL FIRING VELOCITY,VO."
165  PRINT
170  PRINT "AND ANGLE OF CANNON ELEVATION, THETA"
200  VTAB 23: PRINT "PRESS ANY KEY TO CONTINUE."
210  GET ANS$
220  REM SET TIME INCREMENT:
230  DT = .1
240    REM SET X BOUNDS:
250  XL = - 100:XH = 100
260    REM SET Y COORDINATE FOR SCREEN BOTTOM
270  YL = 0
280  S = .625 : REM SCALE FACTOR
290    REM COMPUTE HIGH Y SO THAT
300    REM (YH - YL)/(XH - XL) = S:
310  YH = S * (XH - XL)
320    HGR
330    VTAB 23
340  PRINT "ENTER X COORDINATE OF CANNON"
350    PRINT : PRINT XL;" < = X < = "; XH
360  INPUT XI
370  PRINT "ENTER Y COORDINATE OF CANNON"
380  PRINT : PRINT YL;"< = Y < = "; YH
390  INPUT YI
400  REM PLOT INITIAL LOCATION:
410  HCOLOR = 3
420  X = XI:Y = YI: GOSUB 760 : REM PLOT
430  PRINT "WHAT FIRING VELOCITY DO YOU WANT";
440  INPUT VO
450  PRINT "WHAT ANGLE OF CANNON ELEVATION"
455  PRINT "DO YOU WANT"
460  INPUT K
470  HOME :VTAB 23
480  PRINT " INITIAL CONDITIONS: ";
490  PRINT "X = "; XI;",Y = "; YI
500  PRINT " VO ="; VO ;", THETA = "; K
502  REM CHANGE THETA DEGREES TO RADIAN
504  PI = 4 * ATN (1)
506  THETA = K * PI / 180
508  VX = VO * COS (THETA)
509  VY = VO * SIN (THETA)
510    REM SET X AND Y ACCELERATIONS:
520  AX = 0
530  AY = - 32: REM FT PER SEC PER SEC
```

```
540   REM WIPE OUT OLD LOCATION:
550   REM HCOLOR = 0:GOSUB 760
560   REM COMPUTE NEW X COORDINATE:
570 X = X + DT * VX
580   REM IF X OUT OF RANGE.END:
590   IF X < XL or X > XH THEN 710
600   REM COMPUTE NEW Y COORDINATE:
610 Y = Y + DT * VY
620   REM IF Y OUT OF RANGE,END:
630   IF Y < YL THEN 710
640   REM COMPUTE NEW X AND Y VELOCITIES:
650 VX = VX + DT * AX
660 VY = VY + DT * AY
670   REM PLOT NEW LOCATION:
680   HCOLOR = 3
690   GOSUB 760 : REM PLOTTER
700   GOTO 540
710   REM HERE POINT IS OFF SCREEN
720   PRINT "OFF SCREEN"
730   PRINT "DO ANOTHER (Y OR N)";:INPUT AN$
740   IF ANS$ <    > "N" THEN 320
750   TEST : HOME : END
760   REM PLOTTER SUBROUTINE
770   REM
780   REM CONVERT X,Y TO U,V:
790   REM
800   REM X = XL TO U = 0
810   REM X = XH TO U = 279
820   REM
830   REM Y = YL TO V = 159
840   REM Y = YH TO V = 0
850   REM
860 U = 279 * (X − XL) / (XH − XL)
870 V = − 159 * (Y − YH) / (YH − YL)
880   REM IF U OR V OUT OF RANGE.RETURN:
890   IF U < 0 OR U > 279 THEN 920
900   IF V < 0 OR V > 159 THEN 920
910   HPLOT U,V
920   RETURN
930   REM
```

REFERENCE

Swetz, Frank J. "An Historical Example of Mathematical Modelling: The Trajectory of a Cannonball." *International Journal of Mathematical Education in Science and Technology* 20 (1989): 731–41.

21. FOOD WEB OF SELECTED ANIMALS

Teacher's Guide

To work with this model, students must be able to multiply and add matrices. This model provides motivation for the discussion of matrix arithmetic commonly found in algebra 2. Popular literature usually discusses food "chains," whereas the concept of food "web" is more relevant to real-world situations. It would be helpful to have a biology teacher give a brief introduction to food-web concepts before the students work on the details.

On questions 2–13, it is suggested that the three-animal food web be discussed with the entire class before the students do the work in small groups.

As an extension and modification of the problem, ask several highly motivated students to analyze the environmental effect of a pollutant that kills the trout, frogs, and crayfish but does not directly affect the insects.

Research verified the relationships in the food web. Although the web represents a small segment of the ecosystem, the model will help students understand how the environment is altered in unexpected ways by human actions.

Solutions to question in the model

1.
$$\begin{bmatrix} 0 & 0 & 1 \\ 0 & 0 & 0 \\ 0 & 0 & 0 \end{bmatrix}$$

2.
$$\begin{bmatrix} 0 & 1 & 0 & 0 & 0 & 1 & 1 \\ 0 & 0 & 1 & 0 & 0 & 0 & 0 \\ 0 & 0 & 1 & 0 & 0 & 0 & 0 \\ 0 & 0 & 1 & 0 & 1 & 0 & 0 \\ 0 & 0 & 1 & 0 & 0 & 0 & 0 \\ 0 & 0 & 1 & 1 & 1 & 0 & 0 \\ 0 & 1 & 0 & 0 & 1 & 0 & 0 \end{bmatrix}$$

No animals rely on bears as a source of food.

3. The row sums in order are 3, 1, 1, 2, 1, 3, 2.

4. More animals rely on insects for food than any other source.

5.
$$\begin{bmatrix} 0 & 1 & 2 & 1 & 1 & 0 & 0 \\ 0 & 0 & 1 & 0 & 0 & 0 & 0 \\ 0 & 0 & 1 & 0 & 0 & 0 & 0 \\ 0 & 0 & 2 & 0 & 0 & 0 & 0 \\ 0 & 0 & 1 & 0 & 0 & 0 & 0 \\ 0 & 0 & 3 & 0 & 1 & 0 & 0 \\ 0 & 0 & 2 & 0 & 0 & 0 & 0 \end{bmatrix}$$

6. $\begin{bmatrix} 0 & 2 & 2 & 1 & 1 & 1 & 1 \\ 0 & 0 & 2 & 0 & 0 & 0 & 0 \\ 0 & 0 & 2 & 0 & 0 & 0 & 0 \\ 0 & 0 & 3 & 0 & 1 & 0 & 0 \\ 0 & 0 & 2 & 0 & 0 & 0 & 0 \\ 0 & 0 & 4 & 1 & 2 & 0 & 0 \\ 0 & 1 & 2 & 0 & 1 & 0 & 0 \end{bmatrix}$; the row sums in order are 8, 2, 2, 4, 2, 7, 4.

7. Bears

8. $\begin{bmatrix} 0 & 1 & 0 & 0 & 0 & 1 & 1 \\ 0 & 0 & 0 & 0 & 0 & 0 & 0 \\ 0 & 0 & 0 & 0 & 0 & 0 & 0 \\ 0 & 0 & 0 & 0 & 1 & 0 & 0 \\ 0 & 0 & 0 & 0 & 0 & 0 & 0 \\ 0 & 0 & 0 & 1 & 1 & 0 & 0 \\ 0 & 1 & 0 & 0 & 1 & 0 & 0 \end{bmatrix}$

9. The row sums of the animals that rely on insects for a source of food have decreased by 1.

10. $\begin{bmatrix} 0 & 1 & 0 & 1 & 2 & 0 & 0 \\ 0 & 0 & 0 & 0 & 0 & 0 & 0 \\ 0 & 0 & 0 & 0 & 0 & 0 & 0 \\ 0 & 0 & 0 & 0 & 0 & 0 & 0 \\ 0 & 0 & 0 & 0 & 0 & 0 & 0 \\ 0 & 0 & 0 & 0 & 1 & 0 & 0 \\ 0 & 0 & 0 & 0 & 0 & 0 & 0 \end{bmatrix}$; $\begin{bmatrix} 0 & 2 & 0 & 1 & 2 & 1 & 1 \\ 0 & 0 & 0 & 0 & 0 & 0 & 0 \\ 0 & 0 & 0 & 0 & 0 & 0 & 0 \\ 0 & 0 & 0 & 0 & 0 & 0 & 0 \\ 0 & 0 & 0 & 0 & 0 & 0 & 0 \\ 0 & 0 & 0 & 1 & 2 & 0 & 0 \\ 0 & 1 & 0 & 0 & 1 & 0 & 0 \end{bmatrix}$

11. The row sums are 7, 0, 0, 1, 0, 3, 2.

12. Yes. The bear will be affected the least.

22. WHICH CUP IS BEST?

Teacher's Guide

This modeling project represents an excellent opportunity for interaction among the physics, the computer science, and the mathematics classes. The physics instructor can discuss heat flow in general, the computer science instructor can assist with implementing a linear-regression software package, and the mathematics teacher can discuss the three function types under consideration so that more valid comparisons can be made. Remind the students to record T_M, or air temperature, before the coffee is poured. Use thermometers that will enable the students to read the temperatures accurately to the nearest $0.1°$.

REFERENCES

Anton, Howard. *Calculus.* New York: John Wiley & Sons, 1986.

Whitmore, David G., and Bruce J. Chalmer. *Statpal—a Statistical Package for Microcomputers.* New York: Marcel Dekker, 1985.

Bibliography for Mathematical Modeling

Agnew, Jeanne, Marvin S. Keener, and Ross L. Finney. "Challenging Applications: Problems in the Raw." *Mathematics Teacher* 76 (April 1983): 274–75.

Anderson, Bill, and John Lamb. "The Mathematical Aspects of a Lunar Shuttle Landing." *Mathematics Teacher* 74 (October 1981): 549–53.

Archer, J. Andrew. "The Shortest Route." *Mathematics Teacher* 80 (February 1987): 88–93, 142.

Arganbright, Deane. "An Optimization Problem and Model." *Mathematics Teacher* 71 (December 1978): 769–73.

Armstrong, Gerald M., and Calvin P. Midgley. "The Exponential-Decay Law Applied to Medical Dosages." *Mathematics Teacher* 80 (February 1987): 110–13.

Ashby, Patricia, Samuel L. Dunn, Ruth Chamberlain, and Kenneth Christensen. "People, People, People." *Mathematics Teacher* 71 (April 1978): 283–90.

Austin, Joe Dan. "Overbooking Airline Flights." *Mathematics Teacher* 75 (March 1982): 221–23.

Austin, Joe Dan, and F. Barry Dunning. "Mathematics of the Rainbow." *Mathematics Teacher* 81 (September 1988): 484–88.

Barrett, Gloria, Dot Doyle, and Dan Teague. "Using Data Analysis in Precalculus to Model Cooling." *Mathematics Teacher* 81 (November 1988): 680–84.

Beckmann, Charlene E. "Interpreting Graphs." *Mathematics Teacher* 81 (May 1989): 353–60.

Bland, Paul, and Betty Givan. "An Analysis of Two Car-buying Strategies." *Mathematics Teacher* 76 (February 1983): 124–27.

Broughton, Peter. "Halley's Comet in the Classroom." *Mathematics Teacher* 79 (February 1986): 85–89.

Burch, Charles J., Jr., and Dan Kunkle. "Modeling Growth—a Discrete Approach." *Mathematics Teacher* 77 (April 1984): 266–68.

Burrill, John C., and Henry S. Kepner, Jr. "Relating Graphs to Their Equations with a Microcomputer." *Mathematics Teacher* 79 (March 1986): 185–97.

Cashing, Douglas L., and Albert White. "The Mathematics of Wrong Turns." *Mathematics Teacher* 79 (November 1986): 615–16.

Christensen, Helen. *Mathematical Modeling for the Marketplace: Graphs and Digraphs in Everyday Life*. Baltimore: Loyola College, 1985.

Committee on Enrichment Models, Mathematical Sciences Department, University of Delaware. *Dynamic Programming—an Elegant Problem Solver*. Contemporary Applied Mathematics, vol. 1. Providence, R.I.: Janson Publications, 1987.

———. *Mathematics and Medicine—How Serious Is the Injury?* Contemporary Applied Mathematics, vol. 2. Providence, R.I.: Janson Publications, 1987.

———. *Glyphs—Getting the Picture*. Contemporary Applied Mathematics, vol. 3. Providence, R.I.: Janson Publications, 1987.

———. *Queues—Will the Wait Never End!* Contemporary Applied Mathematics, vol. 4. Providence, R.I.: Janson Publications, 1987.

———. *Graph Theory—Euler's Rich Legacy*. Contemporary Applied Mathematics, vol. 5. Providence, R.I.: Janson Publications, 1987.

———. *Graphical Estimation*. Providence, R.I.: Janson Publications, forthcoming.

———. *Information Theory*. Providence, R.I.: Janson Publications, 1987.

———. *Introduction to Cluster Analysis with Applications.* Providence, R.I.: Janson Publications, forthcoming.

———. *Introduction to Statistical Bootstrapping.* Providence, R.I.: Janson Publications, forthcoming.

———. *Mathematical Theory of Search.* Providence, R.I.: Janson Publications, forthcoming.

Consortium for Mathematics and Its Applications. Applications of Intermediate Algebra. UMAP Module, pack A. Arlington, Mass.: COMAP, n.d.

———. Applications of Arithmetic. UMAP Module, pack B. Arlington, Mass.: COMAP, n.d.

———. Applications of Calculus. UMAP Module, pack C. Arlington, Mass.: COMAP, n.d.

———. *Consortium: The Newsletter of the Consortium for Mathematics and Its Applications.* 60 Lowell St., Arlington, MA 02174. (Quarterly)

———. *Introduction to Contemporary Mathematics.* Telecourse. Arlington, Mass.: Consortium for Mathematics and Its Applications, 1989.

Copes, Wayne, William Sacco, and John W. Jameson. "Queues and Simulations for Secondary School Students." *Mathematics Teacher* 79 (May 1986): 343–47.

Cozgens, Margaret, and Richard Porter. *Recurrence Relations—Counting Backwards.* HiMAP Modules, No. 2. Arlington, Mass.: COMAP, 1985.

Daniels, David. "Fast Brakes." *Mathematics Teacher* 82 (February 1989): 104–7, 111.

Duncan, David R., and Bonnie H. Litwiller. "Apportionment Examples: An Application of Decimal Ordering." *Mathematics Teacher* 76 (February 1983): 89–91.

———. "Turning Landslides into Cliffhangers: An Analysis of Presidential Election Returns." *Mathematics Teacher* 79 (November 1986): 605–8.

Dym, Clive L., and Elizabeth S. Ivey. *Principles of Mathematical Modeling.* Orlando, Fla.: Academic Press, 1980.

Ecker, Michael W. "Getting the Bigger Picture." *Mathematics Teacher* 75 (October 1982): 582.

Eisner, Milton P. "An Application of Quadratic Equations to Baseball." *Mathematics Teacher* 79 (May 1986): 327–30.

Esty, Edward, and James Czepiel. "Mathematics in the Newspaper." *Mathematics Teacher* 73 (November 1980): 582–86.

Ewbank, William. "A Matter of Disks." *Mathematics Teacher* 79 (February 1986): 96–97.

———. "The Summer Olympic Games: A Mathematical Opportunity." *Mathematics Teacher* 77 (May 1984): 344–48.

Fawcett, George. "Camera Calculations." *Mathematics Teacher* 74 (May 1981): 366–67, 398.

Feltman, James. "Cryptics and Statistics." *Mathematics Teacher* 72 (March 1979): 189–91.

Fiore, Gregory. "An Application of Linear Equations to the VCR." *Mathematics Teacher* 81 (October 1988): 570–72.

Frank, Kenneth. "Bent Wire—an Application of Quadratic Equations and Inequalities." *Mathematics Teacher* 79 (February 1986): 57–58.

Fremont, Herbert. *Teaching Secondary Mathematics through Applications.* Boston: Prindle, Weber & Schmidt, 1979.

Garman, Brian. "Applying a Linear Function to Schedule Tennis Matches." *Mathematics Teacher* 77 (October 1984): 544–47.

Gibson, Edwin C., and Jane B. Gibson. "I Can See Clearly Now (Another Look at Norman Windows)." *Mathematics Teacher* 75 (November 1982): 694–97.

Giordano, Frank R., and Maurice Weir. *A First Course in Mathematical Modeling.* Monterey, Calif.: Brooks/Cole Publishing Co., 1985.

Gonzales, Michael G., and William J. Carr. "Impact of the Black Death (1348–1405) on World Population: Then and Now." *Mathematics Teacher* 79 (February 1986): 92–94, 146.

Graening, Jay. "The Geometry of Tennis." *Mathematics Teacher* 75 (November 1982): 658–63.

Growney, JoAnne S. *Using Percent.* HiMAP Modules, No. 5. Arlington, Mass.: COMAP, 1987.

Guillotte, Henry P. "The Method of Finite Differences: Some Applications." *Mathematics Teacher* 79 (September 1986): 466–70.

Harmeyer, Kathleen M. "Flying in Algebra Class." *Mathematics Teacher* 75 (March 1982): 224–26. (See also "High Flying," October 1982, p. 544.)

Harris, Whitney, Jr. "The Corner Reflector." *Mathematics Teacher* 76 (February 1983): 92–95.

Hauser, Larry L. "Baseball Monte Carlo Style." *Mathematics Teacher* 74 (May 1981): 340–41.

Henningsen, Jacqueline. "An Activity for Predicting Performance in the 1984 Summer Olympics." *Mathematics Teacher* 77 (May 1984): 338–41.

Holftan, Boyd. "Please Check Your Telephone Directory." *Mathematics Teacher* 79 (February 1986): 104–6.

Iannone, Michael A. "Round Robin Schedules." *Mathematics Teacher* 76 (March 1983): 194–95.

Jeffrey, Neil J. "Mathematical Photography." *Mathematics Teacher* 73 (December 1980): 657–62.

Johnson, Alonzo F. "The Rule of 78: A Rule That Outlived Its Useful Life." *Mathematics Teacher* 81 (September 1988): 450–53, 480.

———. "The t in $I = Prt$." *Mathematics Teacher* 75 (October 1982): 595–97.

Kastner, Bernice. *Space Mathematics*. Washington, D.C.: National Aeronautics and Space Administration, 1985.

Kennedy, Dan. "Mathematics in the Real World, Really." *Mathematics Teacher* 78 (January 1985): 18–22. (See also "Price Wars," November 1985, p. 588.)

Kememy, John G., and J. Laurie Shell. *Mathematical Models in the Social Sciences*. Blaisdell Publishing Co., 1962.

Kluepfel, Charles. "When Are Logarithms Used?" *Mathematics Teacher* 74 (April 1981): 250–52.

Knill, George. "Baseball and the Midway." *Mathematics Teacher* 74 (April 1981): 286–87.

———. "Cloud Height at Night." *Mathematics Teacher* 73 (October 1980): 508–10.

———. "Estimating the Size of Wildlife Population." *Mathematics Teacher* 74 (October 1981): 548, 571.

———. "Fingerprints and Fractions." *Mathematics Teacher* 73 (November 1980): 608–9.

———. "Light My Fire." *Mathematics Teacher* 75 (January 1982): 53.

———. "Mathematics in Forensic Medicine." *Mathematics Teacher* 74 (February 1981): 126, 149.

———. "The Mathematics of Sight." *Mathematics Teacher* 74 (November 1981): 636–37.

———. "Skid Marks Estimate Speed." *Mathematics Teacher* 74 (December 1981): 722–24.

———. "The Telephone Rate Grid." *Mathematics Teacher* 73 (September 1980): 454–56.

———. "This Is Your Life." *Mathematics Teacher* 75 (February 1982): 144–45.

Krause, Eugene F. "Central-Point Problems." *Mathematics Teacher* 75 (March 1982): 198–202.

———. "Some Applications of the Circumference Formula." *Mathematics Teacher* 75 (May 1982): 369–77.

Lamb, John F., Jr., and Bill D. Anderson. "The Mathematical Aspects of a Lunar Shuttle Landing." *Mathematics Teacher* 74 (October 1981): 549–53.

Lamb, John F., Jr., Bill D. Anderson, and Dennis P. Grantham. "Mathematical Aspects of a Lunar Shuttle Landing Revisited." *Mathematics Teacher* 77 (September 1984): 460–64.

Landwehr, James M., and Ann E. Watkins. "Stem-and-Leaf Plots." *Mathematics Teacher* 78 (October 1985): 528–38.

Li Changming. "A Geometric Solution to a Problem of Minimization." *Mathematics Teacher* 81 (January 1988): 61–64.

Maier, Eugene. "Counting Pizza Pieces and Other Combinatorial Problems." *Mathematics Teacher* 81 (January 1988): 22–26.

Malkevitch, Joseph. *The Mathematical Theory of Elections.* HiMAP Modules, No. 1. Arlington, Mass.: COMAP, 1985.

Mansheim, Jan, and Phyllis Baldridge. "Three Methods of Attacking Problems in Discrete Mathematics, Part 1." *Mathematics Teacher* 80 (March 1987): 224–30.

———. "Three Methods of Attacking Problems in Discrete Mathematics, Part 2." *Mathematics Teacher* 80 (April 1987): 282–88.

Martin, W. Gary, and João Ponte. "Measuring the Area of Golf Greens and Other Irregular Regions." *Mathematics Teacher* 78 (May 1985): 385–89.

Metz, James. "Slope as Speed." *Mathematics Teacher* 81 (April 1988): 285–89.

Mizrahi, Abe, and Michael Sullivan. *Finite Mathematics with Applications for Business and Social Sciences.* New York: John Wiley & Sons, 1973.

Nievergelt, Yves. "Fishers' Effect: Real Growth Is Not Interest Less Inflation." *Mathematics Teacher* 81 (October 1988): 546–47.

———. "Functions Give Three Points of View on the New Income Tax Law." *Mathematics Teacher* 81 (March 1989): 176–81.

Noone, E. T. "Chuck-a-Luck: Learning Probability Concepts with Games of Chance." *Mathematics Teacher* 81 (February 1988): 121–23.

Olson, Alton T. "Building Birdhouses with Vectors and Linear Homogeneous Equations." *Mathematics Teacher* 74 (April 1981): 288–92.

———. "Difference Equations." *Mathematics Teacher* 81 (October 1988): 540–44.

O'Shea, Thomas. "Dirichlet Polygons—an Example of Geometry in Geography." *Mathematics Teacher* 79 (March 1986): 170–73.

Ott, Jack A. "Who's Going to Win the Playoff?" *Mathematics Teacher* 78 (October 1985): 559–63.

Ott, Jack A., and Anthony Contento. "Where Is the Ball Going?" *Mathematics Teacher* 79 (September 1986): 456–60.

Palmaccio, Richard J. "Shipboard Weather Observation." *Mathematics Teacher* 76 (March 1983): 165–68.

Pancari, John, and John P. Pace. "Two Views of Oz." *Mathematics Teacher* 80 (February 1987): 100–101.

Parzynski, William R. "The Geometry of Microwave Antennas." *Mathematics Teacher* 77 (April 1984): 294–96.

Ptak, Dave. "Probability and the Seating Chart." *Mathematics Teacher* 81 (May 1988): 393–97.

Rector, Robert E. "Game Theory: An Application of Probability." *Mathematics Teacher* 80 (February 1987): 138–42.

Reesink, Carole J. "Geomegy and Geolotry: What Happens When Geology Visits Geometry Class?" *Mathematics Teacher* 75 (September 1982): 454–61.

Riley, James E., and Ruth Ann Meyer. "Transportation—a Rich Source of Story Problems." *Mathematics Teacher* 74 (March 1981): 180–83, 240.

Roberti, Joseph. "Interdimensional Relationships." *Mathematics Teacher* 81 (February 1988): 96–100.

Ruppel, Elizabeth. "Business Formulas for Cartesian Curves." *Mathematics Teacher* 75 (May 1982): 398–403.

Saunders, Hal. "When Are We Ever Gonna Have to Use This?" *Mathematics Teacher* 73 (January 1980): 7–16. (See also "Drug Dosages," May 1980, p. 324, and "Word Problems," October 1980, p. 487.)

Schuster, Richard E., and Francisco deP. Soler. "Compound Growth and Related Situations: A Problem-solving Approach." *Mathematics Teacher* 75 (November 1982): 640–44.

Schwartzman, Steven. "On Population and Resources." *Mathematics Teacher* 76 (November 1983): 605–8.

———. "Serendipity: Batting Averages to Greatest Integer." *Mathematics Teacher* 73 (April 1980): 278–80.

Shulte, Albert, and Jim Swift. "Data Fitting without Formulas." *Mathematics Teacher* 79 (April 1986): 264–71.

Shyers, Joan H. "You Can't Get There from Here—an Algorithmic Approach to Eulerian and Hamiltonian Circuits." *Mathematics Teacher* 80 (February 1987): 95–98.

Sloyer, Clifford. *Fantastiks of Mathematiks*. Providence, R.I.: Janson Publications, 1986.

Sloyer, Clifford, Richard Crouse, William Sacco, and Wayne Copes. "Dynamic Programming for Secondary School Students." *Mathematics Teacher* 78 (February 1985): 132–36, 145.

Sloyer, Clifford, and William Sacco. "An Application of the Distance Formula to Medical Science." *Mathematics Teacher* 77 (January 1984): 27–29.

Spence, Lawrence E. "Revisiting Some Counting Problems in Discrete Mathematics." *Mathematics Teacher* 81 (March 1988): 183–86.

Stensholt, Boonchai Kuekiatngam, and Eivind Stensholt. "Invertible Points of Time." *Mathematics Teacher* 81 (April 1988): 304–5.

Sterba, Don. "Probability and Basketball." *Mathematics Teacher* 74 (November 1981): 624–27, 681.

Sterrett, Andrew. "Electing a President in a Three-Candidate Race." *Mathematics Teacher* 73 (November 1980): 635.

Sullivan, John J. "Apportionment—a Decennial Problem." *Mathematics Teacher* 75 (January 1982): 20–25. (See also "Members as Fractions," April 1982, p. 283, and "2/3 of 19," October 1982, pp. 540–41.)

Swetz, Frank J. "An Historical Example of Mathematical Modelling: The Trajectory of a Cannonball." *International Journal of Mathematical Education in Science and Technology* 20 (1989): 731–41.

———. "Mathematics: A Vehicle for Better Global Understanding." *Mathematics Teacher* 78 (November 1985): 207–15.

———. "When and How Can We Use Modeling?" *Mathematics Teacher* 82 (December 1989): 722–26.

Taffe, William J. "Mathematics in a Pumpkin Patch." *Mathematics Teacher* 71 (October 1979): 603–7.

Tisdale, Joseph C. III. "An Interest in Interest." *Mathematics Teacher* 82 (February 1989): 126–27.

Vest, Floyd. "Modeling the Cost of Homeownership." *Mathematics Teacher* 79 (November 1986): 610–13.

———. "Secondary School Mathematics from the EPA Gas Mileage Guide." *Mathematics Teacher* 72 (January 1979): 10–14. (See also "EPA Gas Mileage," May 1979, p. 322.)

Wagner, Clifford H. "Determining Fuel Consumption—an Exercise in Applied Mathematics." *Mathematics Teacher* 72 (February 1979): 134–36.

Wagner, Leonard M. "Modeling with Difference Equations: Two Examples." *Mathematics Teacher* 77 (February 1984): 136–40.

Wallace, Edward. "Using Linear Functions." *Mathematics Teacher* 81 (October 1988): 560–66.

Wood, Eric F. "Mathematics and Meteorology." *Mathematics Teacher* 79 (November 1986): 602–3.

———. "Self-checking Codes—an Application of Modular Arithmetic." *Mathematics Teacher* 80 (April 1987): 312–16.

Woodrow Wilson National Fellowship Foundation. *Mathematical Modeling*. Princeton, N.J.: The Foundation, 1988.

Woodward, Ernest, and Thomas Hamel. "Calculator Lessons Involving Population, Inflation, and Energy." *Mathematics Teacher* 72 (September 1979): 450–57.

Woods, Jimmy C. "Maximum Profit without Calculus." *Mathematics Teacher* 81 (March 1988): 224–26.

Zagare, Frank C. *The Mathematics of Conflict*. HiMAP Modules, no. 3. Arlington, Mass.:
    COMAP, 1985.
Zitarelli, David E. "Prediction Runs." *Mathematics Teacher* 75 (March 1982): 236–37, 247.
    (See also "Harmonic Means," September 1982, p. 440.)